'This is a book of real and rare enchantment, simply written about simple and primitive things, without any touch of affectation.'
Sunday Times

'A miracle...the book is an enchanting one and almost reconciles one to being a human being.'
TLS

'An astonishing book, a gem of purest ray, serene...This is a wonderful book: and I mean just that—it is full of wonder...'
Evening News

'One of the most enchanting animal books for years.'
The Star

'A graceful and essentially honest book. Rowena Farre does not romanticise the wilderness, nor braggingly dramatise the toughness of their Cold Comfort Farm. Yet the plain fabric of their life through the changing seasons makes one's own metropolitan busy-ness seem a shoddy and pointless rat-race.'
Kenneth Allsop, *Daily Mail*

'If there is much that is lighthearted...there is also much to tell us how deeply the author entered into the spirit of the austere land.'
The Scots Magazine

Seal
Morning

the author

Rowena Farre was born in India, where she spent the early years of her life. She later moved to Scotland to live with her aunt, travelled around Britain with gypsies and undertook a spiritual journey to the Himalayas. *Seal Morning* was her first autobiographical work, followed by *A Time from the World* and *The Beckoning Land*. She died aged 57 in 1979.

Seal
Morning
ROWENA FARRE

afterword
by
Maurice Fleming

BIRLINN

First Published by Hutchinson & Co (Publishers) Ltd. in 1957
This edition published in 2001 by Mercat Press
and reprinted in 2003
Reprinted in 2008 and 2013 by Birlinn Limited
West Newington House
10 Newington Road
Edinburgh
EH9 1QS

www.birlinn.co.uk

ISBN: 978 1 84158 690 8

British Library Cataloguing-in-Publication Data
A catalogue record for this book is available from the
British Library

Set in Utopia at Mercat Press

Printed and bound by Grafica Veneta
www.graficaveneta.com

contents

the wilderness

The county of Sutherland is composed for the greater part of moor, bog, and water. Trees are a rarity; birch and pine scatter the moors singly or in small groups. Out-crops of rock, often weathered to strange shapes, are strewn over the landscape. When a storm is approaching, or in the half-light, the effect of this boulder-strewn landscape is eerie and to some people even frightening.

After twenty years as a teacher in one of the Home Counties my Aunt Miriam, with whom I lived, decided to give up her career and return to her native Scotland. Her original plan had been to buy a small house near Inverness, where she had lived as a girl, but on hearing of a croft for sale at a moderate price in a particularly remote and barren part of Sutherland her pioneering spirit got the better of her, and, against the advice of friends and relations, she bought the place.

The croft possessed no conveniences ancient or modern. Lighting was by paraffin lamps. Water had to be carried in buckets from a stream. There was, of course, no telephone. To get medical aid entailed a journey on foot or by trap to the nearest *clachan*, or village, some nine miles away, to put through a call to a township, for no doctor or nurse lived in the clachan.

A path, little better than a sheep-track, wound from our door over the moors. It gradually merged into an unsurfaced road, and for the last four miles, before entering the clachan, there was actually a coating of tarmac on it. During winter, stretches of this road would be covered in deep snowdrifts making travel along it impossible for weeks at a time. In late autumn we would get in a good supply of stores to tide us over the bad patches when we were snowbound.

Behind us we left a countryside of trim fields and tall elms under which drowsed placid cattle, and we installed ourselves in an area where to ignore the white heads of cottongrass which sway over the bogs, or to fail to take one's bearings in an oncoming mist, could mean death. The move to our new abode took three weeks to accomplish. Every stick of furniture and piece of baggage, including an upright piano, had to be transported over the last six miles in a farm wagon. Besides the baggage and furniture, we also brought with us two grey squirrels and a weakly specimen of *rattus norvegicus*, i.e. a common brown rat. This latter had been presented to Aunt Miriam just before we left our snug, orchard-bound cottage by one of her former pupils.

"I do hope you won't take his gift the wrong way, Miss Farre. He knows you are very fond of animals," the anxious father of the donator had thought well to explain. Aunt accepted Rodney in the spirit in which he was given, and passed him on to me.

Of all the animals I have reared I can think of none which has given me more trouble than this ratling. His mouth being too tiny for the insertion of an old-fashioned pen-dipper, I was compelled to administer milk at all hours of the day and night by means of a piece of screwed up cottonwool, making sure that in his efforts to suck out the milk he did not swallow any of the wool. By the time we had settled into the croft his health, somewhat to my pride, was less precarious, and the natural energy and inquisitiveness possessed to a greater or lesser degree by all healthy animals were beginning to animate his behaviour. He soon became adept at climbing the parlour curtains and showed much interest in going over the contents of the sewing basket. Indeed, Rodney came near to being a full day's work.

An ardent lover in any sphere of life cannot go long unde- tected, and within a week of arriving at the croft we received a visit from our nearest neighbour—a shepherd who lived four miles away. He carried in his arms a pair of otter cubs as a present for Aunt. The news had already reached him that she was 'fond of animals.'

As well as the feeding of ourselves, which we found quite a problem at first in these remote parts, we also had to sat- isfy the voracious appetites of the animals. It was almost frightening to watch the otter cubs race through their meal of homemade brown bread and milk laced with oil, and, having licked clean the plate, look round for more. Rodney too, hav- ing started life with a negligible appetite, began to develop an alarming one for so small a creature. His main dish con- sisted of the same fare as the otters without the addition of oil, but fruit, vegetables, cakes, chocolates and biscuits went down equally well. To stave off the pangs of hunger between meals he took to climbing into the wastepaper basket and chewing up old envelopes. Fortunately for us, as they grew older, all our animals became largely self-supporting where food was concerned, the otters catching fish in the numer- ous streams and the nearby *lochan* (small loch). Our days began to run to a pattern of rising, tending the animals, breakfast, my lessons—I was ten when I went to live in the croft—carrying in the day's supply of water, cooking, walks over the magnificent countryside during summer, a trip to the clachan once a fortnight to collect provisions in the small pony trap we had bought, and in the evenings strumming on the piano and reading. When I first came to these wild parts there was one thing which impressed itself most forcibly on my consciousness, and which still remains my most potent memory of them. That was the silence. It was a permanent, living silence. Thunder, driving rain, and keening wind were sounds which seemed to emanate from it and fade back into it. Sometimes, particularly on a hot summer's day, it could be sensed in its profundity for the space of a few seconds, unbroken by so much as a crepitation or stirring of wind. At other moments the sudden bark of a deer or cry of a whaup only served to emphasise its depth. It was a vast, unseen but ever present reality.

The croft consisted of a kitchen-cum-parlour, a small bedroom apiece, and a tiny room which was used as a workroom, or a guest room when we had visitors. All the rooms were on the ground floor, there being no upper storey. Outside, within a few yards of the croft, was a partitioned byre. One side was the pony's quarters and the other was used for storing drums of paraffin, bins of grain, tinned food, and the animals' biscuits and fodder. Strangely enough, one of the things we had to do without during the first months of our arrival was fresh milk. The shepherd, Mr. McNairn, kept a cow and would have been willing to sell us a measure of milk each day, but to walk eight miles a day for a can of milk seemed a somewhat extravagant waste of time, so we made do with skimmed and condensed. Later on two goats were added to the livestock and thenceforth we did not lack for fresh milk. Though when we first acquired them, inexpert milker that I was, it struck me not infrequently that perhaps after all it would have been quicker to walk to our neighbour's croft to collect it. Gradually we and the animals began to adapt ourselves to the new surroundings.

It had seemed likely that, with streams and the lochan so close, the otter cubs on growing older would quickly return to their natural life. We made it a rule not to keep an animal if it wished to leave us, unless it had received some injury or was sickly. Otters are great wanderers and travel for miles over the countryside, swimming and on foot. They prefer, though, to travel long distances at night. Hansel and Gretel, however, as I had inappropriately named them, seldom wandered far from the croft that first summer, and always returned dutifully each evening. At nights they slept in a straw-lined box in the parlour.

The squirrels, Cuthbert and Sara, took quite a while to adapt themselves to this strange wilderness to which we had brought them. The sight of the wide open spaces filled them with alarm and sent them bolting through the door and into their wicker cage on the slightest provocation. Gradually they became bolder and took to climbing on to the thatched roof of the croft, which soon became their favourite playground. Here they were often joined by Rodney. Cuthbert, the male squirrel, developed an unfortunate habit of sitting on the chimney. We kept a fire in the range day and night, winter and summer. As he peered down the hole or warmed himself in chill weather on the heated bricks he would become drugged by the smoke, topple over, and come hurtling on to the range. Although he singed his coat badly on two occasions and sustained minor shocks, it took an even bitterer experience than these before he lived and learnt to avoid the chimney. On this third occasion, he landed slap into a saucepan of porridge which, though hot, had luckily not come to the boil. He was a sorry mess when I plucked him out and my ministrations on his behalf in the form of a bath and brisk rub-down were not appreciated. But after that tumble he left the chimney severely alone.

The first winter in our new home was a particularly exhausting one. For days at a time we were unable to leave the croft because of the heavy falls of snow. Then the fuel ran out and for close on a week we had no fires or hot meals. The snow was succeeded by fierce winds and heavy downpours. The hours of daylight were brief. Often the darkness extended past noon and we were cooking the lunch by lamplight. By half-past four it was growing dark again.

In June of the following year I left to spend a holiday with friends on the isle of Lewis in the Outer Hebrides. The weather throughout my stay was very rough. Walking along the beach one morning to collect pieces of driftwood, I saw a fisherman coming towards me carrying an oddly shaped creature in his arms. He told me it was a young seal which had probably got washed off its rock during the night by the gale and separated from its mother. Many young seals are lost in this manner. What was a little unusual was the fact that it was a Common Seal, a species more often found on the East Coast, the Hebrides being the breeding ground of the larger, less intelligent Atlantic Seal. Although my knowledge of seal upbringing was of the scantiest, I promptly asked the fisherman if I might have it, and, greatly to my joy, he placed the seal in my arms. A bottle was presented to me by a kindly woman and I was instructed how to fill it with warmed milk mixed with a little oil. Seals' milk is very rich, containing almost ten times more fat than cows' milk. Lora, as I had named her, took to the bottle without fuss and showed every prospect of thriving. She became very tame almost from the start and enjoyed being handled and stroked.

Animal lover though I knew Aunt Miriam to be, I decided after some thought not to inform her in my letter that I had become the owner of a young Common Seal, but to take my pet back unannounced as a 'surprise', trusting that Lora's affectionate nature would win Aunt over to the realisation that a home without a seal lacks a vital member of the family party. A fortnight later I set off on the two days' journey home with Lora, a somewhat bulky parcel weighing over thirty-eight pounds, wrapped up in a tartan rug.

bringing up a seal

"There are few eyes in the orbits of men and women which suggest more pleasantly the ancient thought of their being windows of the soul. The lids of the eyes are fringed with long, perfect lashes. The mothers' eyes are large, lustrous, blue-blackish and are humid and soft with the tenderest expressions... In the case of the adult males, the light framework of the skull supports an expressive pair of large, bluish-hazel eyes; alternately burning with revengeful passionate light, then suddenly changing to the tones of tenderness and good nature."

This piece of flattery was not penned in admiration of the eyes of a section of the human race, as might be supposed, but in admiration of those of the seal tribe, and was written by a nineteenth century American naturalist, Henry Wood Elliott, who was a great lover of seals and devoted most of his life to their study. That short extract is typical of his writing, much of which is devoted to extolling the seals' virtues. It is a fact that seals have most beautiful and expressive eyes. Even as a pup Lora learnt to use hers with telling effect. A look from her was enough to send me running to fill her bottle or make me aware that she wished to be picked up. Aunt Miriam too, having stated categorically on my arrival home that the pup must be taken back to the sea directly she was able to fend for herself, was won over by Lora in a few days, and much to my relief the subject of her eventual departure from our midst was not mentioned again. But already, though we were unaware of it then, we had left her return to her natural element too late to be accomplished satisfactorily, even had we wished it, for seals, when adopted and reared by hand, become devoted to their human owners and more affectionate than dogs. If taken out to sea in a boat and dropped over the side a seal will follow the vessel or, if the owners manage to make a getaway unnoticed, the deserted creature, in spite of its slow gait, will often travel miles overland in an attempt to find its old home.

Bringing up a seal was no light task, as I was soon to discover. Left on her own for a while Lora would start the curious baaing sound that young seals make, and should no one hasten to her this would change to plaintive whining interspersed with angry barks, which would be kept up until she was given attention. As a pup she had a bottle four times a day. My first mistake in seal upbringing was to allow her to have it on my lap. This privilege once accorded she had no intention of relinquishing it without a tussle. Even when fully grown, measuring some three-and-a-half feet and tipping the scales at over three hundredweight she would still try and scramble up on to a stranger's lap should he or she be weak enough to allow her to do so. Once on my return from a walk I went into the parlour to find Lora entrenched on a breathless and terrified lady visitor.

"She started to bark each time I tried to make her get down and … I wasn't sure if seals bit, so I didn't push her too hard," I was informed. I promptly ordered a reluctant Lora on to the floor.

Allowing her to sleep at the bottom of my bed was another mistake. A seal pup on one's feet is one thing, but a fully-grown seal quite another. It took me several weeks to train her to lie on a low bamboo couch at nights and to refrain from surreptitiously trying to clamber back on to the bed. When on dry land seals move by pulling themselves along on their flippers. No sooner was she past infancy than Lora started to waddle after me round the croft and trail me over to the byre. If I set out on a walk her wails of protest at being left behind would pursue me into the distance. I decided that I must train her to become more independent and capable of amusing herself. We possessed a small rowboat which was kept in a sheltered inlet of the lochan. One day, seeing that the weather was not likely to turn squally, I took her out in it and dropped her over the side. In a moment, she was swimming vigorously, diving, twisting, and circling the boat with incredible swiftness. From a slow-moving, awkward creature she had turned into one of the utmost grace and speed. Each day henceforth she spent many hours swimming with the otters in the lochan. Should we want her, a call from us would usually bring her to the shore. Seals have no ear conches yet they possess very acute hearing.

Now that she had discovered her true element and was growing older our food problem was eased considerably, for she hunted her own fish. The natural diet of seals is crustaceans and fish. But, like most domesticated animals, Lora's taste ranged beyond the natural and she was not averse to a raw carrot, porridge, and, as an occasional treat, a spoonful of oil from a sardine tin. At nights she had a supper consisting of dog biscuits soaked in milk and oil.

Training animals who live in one's own home is somewhat akin to training children; each individual must learn to fit into the life of the household, scope must be given for particular talents to develop, and allowances made for varying degrees of intelligence. In the case of a highly intelligent animal like the Common Seal, elementary training is quick and easy. Lora soon learnt that her mackintosh was kept on a lower shelf of the dresser and that when she came in from the lochan she must sit on it. When still a pup she would bark for one of us to lay it out for her. As she grew older she taught herself to pull it off the shelf and to spread it out fairly adequately on the floor. As seals have stiff, shiny hairs, most of the water pours off them directly they emerge and the drying process is comparatively short. Obedient in many ways and quick to learn, Lora's inquisitive nature got her into trouble more than once. Anything a little strange or new had to be investigated. Thus she would pull at the tablecloth and bring down a shower of cutlery and glasses. The squirrel's cage had eventually to be hung up out of her reach, for she was always pushing her nose through the small door, which was kept tied back, and the squirrels until they had got used to her presence, would be driven into a frenzy of alarm. During a particularly good relay of an opera she knocked over the battery wireless set, and before Aunt Miriam could reach it a knob was almost torn from its socket. This meant five weeks for us without a set. These sort of misdeeds had to be stopped. We tried to steer her avid curiosity into more fruitful channels.

I am against teaching animals tricks, but I see no reason why domestic animals should not be taught to be useful in ways which do not go contrary to their natures. I began teaching Lora to fetch and carry different objects and to take the mail from the postman. The post was delivered twice a week. There was a box set on a short pole about two miles on the track from us. Here we were supposed to collect it, but the postman being a sociable soul, as are most in these parts, generally walked the odd two miles to the croft for a chat and a cup of tea. It was not long before Lora learnt to know on what days he arrived and at approximately what time. Directly she caught sight of his figure coming up the hill she would start towards him. On meeting, he would place the letters in her mouth and she would follow after in his wake. Delivery was apt to be a little tardy over the last lap. There was one unfortunate occasion when, busy over the teacups we did not notice her progress, and halfway to the croft, she decided to go for a swim in the lochan taking the mail with her. Needless to mention, that bundle of letters was lost for ever and aye.

What gave her especial delight was to be allowed to un-pack the shopping basket when we returned from a trip to the clachan or township. Tins would be lifted out carefully and if round, rolled across the floor; exciting looking packages would be shaken hard. Even such mundane objects as dusters and washing-up mops would be sniffed and closely inspected. The basket emptied at last, she would carry it to its place by the kitchen cupboard.

The croft stood in a little oasis of emerald grass. This green-ery extended for about five yards in front before meeting with the heather. To the rear of the croft was a clearing of earth for the growing of a few vegetables, and this was ringed with the grass which acted as a slight barrier against the moorland. Stones seemed to grow like weeds in this tiny patch of ground wrested from the wilderness. Every so often we went over it with hoe and spade to clear it of yet more stones. In the 'garden' we started to grow quite a variety of vegetables; radishes, lettuce, spinach, cabbages and leeks. Potatoes did not do well, seldom reaching a worthwhile size and remaining green. Perhaps the earth did not go deep enough for them. So we gave up planting these. They became a subsidiary item of our meals, bread and oats being our mainstay. A kindly and valiant friend came to stay with us for a week bringing with her a quantity of roots and herb cuttings, together with a stack of heavy flower pots to plant them in. Unfortunately there was no earth to spare from the garden so we had to dig for it on the moors. Hard labour with a vengeance. When there was a tidy mound, the earth was sieved through a coarse sieve to get rid of the ubiquitous stones. The cuttings meanwhile were being kept alive—we hoped—in a bowl of water. When there was a sufficient quantity of sieved earth we potted them and trusted they would 'take'. Surprisingly enough, several sprigs and roots did take, and later on we were able to vary our somewhat monotonous diet by adding herbs and herb sauces. In winter we brought the pots in and ranged them against the sill. No matter what the weather might get up to outside we could still pick parsley to make a savoury porridge, and a sprig of thyme and leaf or two of lemon verbena for an oatmeal sweet.

During our first summer we began to collect large stones in order to make a wall round the garden to act as a break from the winds and as an obstruction to the rabbits. We piled the stones one on top of another until the wall was about three feet in height and two feet thick. Inside this barricade we fixed wire-netting as an additional protection against the rabbits. We soon found that the wall itself, which completely enclosed the garden, was no good at all as a means of keeping the pests at bay. Apart from their burrowing skill, the rabbits were also expert climbers and would have made worthy members of the Alpine Club. They thought nothing of scrambling up the loosely laid wall and springing down to the other side. When we had the netting fixed we believed that that would foil them, as it was cunningly placed several feet away from the wall, leaving a gap of no man's land in between. Any rabbit which jumped down now would find itself in the run, cut off from the vegetables, or so we thought. But a few worthy members of the rabbit tribe managed to prove us wrong. One morning we were nonplussed on seeing a rabbit devouring a young lettuce. We gave chase at once but our quarry escaped through the back door, which we had thoughtlessly left open, and out via the front. A thorough search revealed no holes under the wire and despairingly we reached the conclusion that as well as scaling the wall it must have scaled the wire too. That being so, we agreed it would be as well not to waste our energy planting vegetables, but to admit that the rabbits had beaten us.

The following morning on getting up I happened to glance through my window and I noticed one sitting on the wall. I began watching it in the hope of discovering how it set about clearing the last fence. And that was literally what it did do. For a moment it seemed to be measuring with its eye the distance between the wall and the netting. Then, with a leap, it was across and had landed in the garden. In the past my only close acquaintance with rabbits had been with a couple of pet angoras whose intelligence had always struck me as being singularly low. But these Sutherland bunnies, I realised, were of a superior order, and not to be compared with the nitwitted, woolly angoras. As I watched the little all-round sportsman take a preliminary nibble at a radish leaf I felt almost willing to let him continue the feast. Then I remembered the many days of hard labour I had spent digging up stones and sowing rows of seeds, and I decided otherwise. Having summoned Aunt Miriam, we once more gave chase, this time with the back door closed. Many minutes of running and jumping over the vegetables—now beginning to look as though a sirocco had blown over them—left us exhausted and angry but the rabbit unconcerned, with its vitality, apparently, unimpaired. Whilst we debated the next move it sat cleaning its face by a cabbage.

"Fetch the landing net," said Aunt Miriam curtly.

This net was used by us to land fish, but I supposed there was no reason why it should not land a rabbit as well. More minutes followed of hectic running and jumping. Eventually the rabbit was cornered and bolted into the net. What now?

"I can't kill him," said Aunt promptly.

Certainly, I could not. We rarely ate meat in spite of being surrounded by game, and a rabbit hot-pot would have been welcome. But not, I believe, a hot-pot made from this rabbit. Even had we been able to bring ourselves to put an end to its life it would have been unlikely that either of us would have relished eating so worthy a foe. Yet it seemed ridiculous to free him after all the trouble he had given us, and allow him the opportunity to make a return visit to the garden. But that is what we did do, tipping him over the wall whence he disappeared into the heather. As we were both too squeamish to twist his neck there seemed nothing else to be done.

Mr. McNairn called later on in the day, and our confession that we had given the rabbit his freedom made him slap his hand on the table with anger.

"A wee twist of its neck or a tap on the head would hae done it—let him loose! If only I'd arrived a while sooner. It's a dog you are wanting, Miss Farre. Rabbits smell a dog same as mice smell a cat and keep away."

"No," said Aunt firmly, "we can't have any more animals. As it is—"

"There's no point in wearing yourselves out over a patch of garden unless you hae a dog to keep the varmints from snitching the greens, is there now? You make him sleep over in the byre and never let him put a foot in the croft. Kept like that he'll be nae trouble to ye."

In due course a yellow mongrel pup, called Ben, arrived. He stood low on the ground, had flop ears, and was barrel chested. But in spite of a somewhat heavy and ungainly build he was fleet of foot. For minutes at a time he would sit on the wall watching for a slight movement in the heather, at which he would spring off and investigate. He proved an excellent deterrent to the rabbits. After his arrival we began to have rabbit on the menu frequently, for whenever he caught one he would bring it back, dead but never badly mauled, and in return for one of its paws and a biscuit he would give up the booty. As well as catching rabbits he became adept at catching the vicious little weasels, and once he returned home with a stoat. His love of the chase eventually proved his undoing. Having no dog companion, Ben took up with the otters who were about the same size as himself. His habits became quite aquatic. He would swim considerable distances after them in the lochan, and when I threw the ball out to them from the boat, he would try to reach it before they did.

As a cat and dog will learn to live peaceably together in a house so will other species of animals. After a week over in the byre Ben had managed without much difficulty, to become a permanent member of the croft, sleeping at nights on the matting in front of the range. During the evenings there would be quite a gathering in the parlour. The larger animals, Lora, Ben and the otters, would put up with the smaller fry with fairly good grace. But during the day, when out in the open, Rodney and the squirrels had to look sharp when the otters or Ben were around. The sight of a rat or squirrel streaking past the croft invariably proved too big a temptation for them to resist, and in spite of our admonishments we were never able to train them not to chase these small creatures.

We had not been long at the croft before I had an experience which made me wary in future of the burns after there had been heavy falls of rain. To the west of us was the mountainous district of the Ben Armine range, dominated by the peak of Ben Armine. To the east were the Knockfin Heights and Cnoc Coirena Fearna. Large tracts of the Ben Armine country and the country to the north consist of deer forest. A forest up here does not mean an area covered by trees, but uncultivated, usually hilly or mountainous country, given over to deer and other game. Rivers and burns criss-cross this countryside. Through the Ben Armine area run the rivers Skinsdale and Blackwater and their many tributaries. To the north the Borrabal Forest is watered by the River Free. Farther north again is a string of lochs, including the beautiful Loch a'Chlair and Baddanloch. A glance at a map of this area will show that the only names here are those of loch, river and hill; it is completely devoid of name of township or clachan. The rain had fallen steadily throughout the night and the following morning.

After lunch the sky cleared and it looked as if the weather had set in for a few hours sunshine. I decided to go fishing for trout in one of the burns. Brown trout were plentiful round here. Taking Ben with me, I started off westwards, climbing steadily. The burn for which I was making was only a yard or so wide and the water, a deep russet through running over peat hags, barely reached my knees. On past occasions I had been fortunate in that more than once a trout had flipped into the landing net. I have never fished for 'sport', only for food, and this being so I had no qualms about using the net instead of the rod and line favoured by sportsmen. The burn when I reached it looked the same as usual. Removing my shoes, I stood in the water, the net held out hopefully. Ben, momentarily tired of hunting, was lying on the bank. Fishing gives ample time for reflection, and my thoughts as I stood there were soon concerned with other matters than the possibility of a catch.

Perhaps ten minutes passed, then glancing up at the heights I saw to my astonishment and terror a great mass of water, like a brown avalanche, coming towards me. In an instant, before there was a chance of getting out of its course, I was knocked down and hurtled forwards. The sky was blotted out and I was tossed and buffeted as though I were a twig. Suddenly I was flung up against a flat rock with a tremendous bump which knocked the little remaining air from my lungs. But my hands instinctively gripped the top of the rock and I began pulling myself upwards. When I had recovered somewhat I stared below at the raging torrent which a moment or two ago had been a gently flowing burn. I looked round for Ben but could not see him and I presumed he must have been drowned in the flood. Over to one side of the rock was high ground, and I managed to jump across the waters to it and reach safety. On the way homewards Ben caught up with me, panting and much excited, his coat wet from the ducking. Somehow he too had got clear of the deluge and reached safety. Apart from the loss of the net and a severe bruising I had got off lightly.

Soon after this incident I began keeping a small book in which I wrote down words which held a definite meaning for various members of our animal fraternity. I excluded only the goats and the pony. Under the heading 'Rodney' I find six words; basket, out, raisins, nuts, roof, and Rodney. When any of these words were spoken to him he would, if in the right mood, act in a definite manner. 'Basket!' for instance, would send him, generally at a snail's pace, into his box filled with dry grass. 'Nuts!' however, would send him running towards the left-hand side of the dresser in which was kept a tin of nuts. 'Raisins!' would have him running eagerly over to the right-hand side in which was kept the tin of raisins. Although the words 'nuts' and 'raisins' sent the squirrels scampering to the dresser in anticipation they were never able to distinguish, as could Rodney, between the two words. On either being spoken they would keep up a brisk scamper, back and forth in front of the dresser, squeaking excitedly, until duly rewarded. So under the separate headings of Cuthbert and Sara the two words are tied and counted as one. Looking through the booklet I find that Lora, as was usual in little tests of this kind, comes off best by a very long way. The total number of words under her column is thirty-five. Here are a few of them: basket (her own bamboo couch); in; out; here; Lora; aunt; Rowena; Ben; Hansel; Gretel; Mr. Dobbie (the postman); boat; swim (this word had the same effect on her as 'walk' has on most dogs and had to be used with discretion); ball; sing; mouth organ; trumpet; stick (a drumstick with which she used to play the xylophone); biscuits; plate (her own plate); mackintosh. Of course, as with the other animals too, there were several words and phrases which held a vague meaning for her and to which she sometimes reacted, but these I did not list. Here are the totals of the rest in order of merit; Gretel, the female otter—eighteen words. Hansel, the male otter—sixteen. Ben—twelve. Cuthbert and Sara—five apiece.

Amongst other things that Lora learnt in her early days was never to leave the boat till told she might do so, for there was a danger of its being overturned, unless Aunt Miriam or I were sitting in the right spot to counterbalance her dive. And she also learnt never to touch the boat whilst swimming under it for the same reason. Before this lesson was firmly instilled, though, she had overturned the boat twice, on both occasions fortunately on a hot summer's day when I was wearing a bathing costume. The lochan was relatively free of weeds but neither Aunt nor I ever swam in it unless the other one was in the boat ready to row over should the swimmer find herself in difficulties.

Sometimes Lora would surface holding a stone in her mouth. Gradually she came to learn that when I said 'Stone!' and pointed with a finger down at the water she was expected to dive for one. Unlike Ben with the rabbits, and regrettably where our larder was concerned, Lora never brought back any fish she had caught. All her catches were gulped down on the spot or else taken on to the shore and eaten there. Not once was I able to extract a fish from her in exchange for a biscuit.

lora and music

Since ancient times it has been known that seals are attracted by music and singing and this fact has been woven into many a legend. And Man has known too of the Common Seal's ability to learn to play different instruments. I have in my possession an eighteenth-century book in which there is an engraving of a Common Seal playing the bagpipes.

Lora's musical talent came out early. Whenever Aunt Miriam or I struck up on the piano the other animals would take no notice. Not so Lora. She would wriggle over to the instrument, lean against it or (more inconveniently) the player's legs, and listen with an expression of intense concentration and joy which was quite flattering, swaying now and then with her whole body to the music. When the music stopped she would sit quietly for several minutes, still under its spell. Her reactions to my singing, however, can only be described as humiliating.

A relation had sent me a mouth organ and book of songs for a birthday present. Thumbing through the book, I decided that I would do a little singing practice each day. For the first session I chose a time when Aunt was out picking wild raspberries and there was not an animal within sight. After a preliminary scale or two, I started off on 'Men of Harlech'. To my annoyance, I heard a loud groan beside me. Looking down, I saw Lora and continued singing. Whereupon she broke into a roar. Seals have perhaps the largest vocal range among mammals. Their repertoire includes grunts, snorts, barks, peculiar mewing, hisses, and a wail which often rises from a deep bass to a treble. The roar turned to a hiss. I still took no notice but my reedy efforts were soon outclassed. Then I had the idea of letting her sing on her own to my accompaniment. During the practice sessions which followed, when I played a simple tune at a fairly slow pace with bars of steadily ascending and descending notes, she made valiant efforts to follow the music in a tuneless wail. A sudden high or low note, or a piece played too quickly, plainly annoyed her, for she would start to grunt and beat about with her fore-flippers—a habit of hers when angry. Within a week she was able to get through 'Baa-baa Black Sheep' and 'Danny Boy' without a break, and was beginning to learn, 'Where my Caravan has Rested'.

She began to pester me for the mouth organ. I was playing it outside the croft one afternoon and, growing weary of the grunts and whines and a heavily whiskered nose pressed against my face every so often as she attempted to wrest it from me, I finally acknowledged defeat and placed it in her mouth. From that moment she considered the mouth organ to be hers. Having gained possession of it, she found to her annoyance that it emitted no sound in spite of being gnawed with vigour. So she started tossing it up into the air and catching it as though it were the ball, and then, her annoyance increasing, rolling on it. All to no effect. Taking the instrument in her mouth once again she gave a loud sigh of desperation. This produced a blast of noise from the mouth organ and galvanised Lora to fresh efforts. I set off for a walk. When I returned in about an hour there were most curious sounds coming from the rear of the croft. Lora had learnt the blow-suck method and there she was, blowing and sucking feebly, in a state of almost complete exhaustion, for she had been doing this, apparently, ever since I had left her. She made no protest when I took the mouth organ from her. From that day onwards it became her favourite toy, replacing in her affections the rubber ball which she shared with the dog and otters. I do not think Mr. Larry Adler would have approved of her playing, but it certainly gave her a great deal of pleasure.

I happened to mention in a letter to an elderly relation of mine that Lora was developing into a remarkable seal and could sing and play the mouth organ. Aunt Felicity was a staunch defender of all animals, wild and domesticated, and sat on numerous committees which saw to their protection and well-being. The merest suspicion in her mind that an animal was being badly treated roused her fighting spirit. Her letter in reply to my own left me in no doubt that she considered I was committing heinous crimes against the hapless Lora.

"Dear Rowena, I was shocked and ashamed to learn from your letter that you of all people, whom I have always considered to be a lover of animals, should be capable of mistreating one so," she began. Then, her anger increasing, she continued —"Zoos are an abomination, circuses are worse ... yet by keeping that seal confined to a croft and only allowing it brief swims in a small loch you prove yourself to be no better than a zoo keeper; and by training it in such unnatural antics as singing and playing on a mouth organ you have sunk to the level of an animal trainer at a circus... Don't go telling me in your next letter that you teach the creature by kindness as I know for a fact that only long hours of forced practice could make it perform such tricks."

I did not mention Lora in my next letter, writing only about such safe subjects as the weather—variable as ever up in these parts—and our amateur attempts at making raspberry jam. Aunt Felicity, though facts were against me no doubt, was quite wide of the mark where Lora's freedom and musical practice were concerned.

At nights Lora slept on her couch in my room. The door of the bedroom was left ajar and the front door was also kept open during the summer so that an animal could get out should it wish to. Most mornings, when breakfast had been eaten and cleared away, and the other animals had long since been out and about, Lora, a late riser, was still dozing on the couch. So it was a surprise when I was woken up very early one morning—it could not have been much later than half-past five—by her flopping off the couch and going into the parlour. The silence was shattered a moment later by hideous blow-suck noises. Her mouth organ had been left on the carpet the night before and it seemed she had decided to put in a little practice on it. Snarls and growls from Ben and the otters proved that they were finding early morning music as uncongenial as I was.

"Take that thing away from her at once!" shouted Aunt Miriam.

I did as I was bidden and placed the mouth organ on the mantelpiece. The whines which followed at having her plaything taken from her were almost as aggravating as the previous cacophony. Eventually she took herself off to the lochan. By then it was time to get up anyway.

A young friend of mine, after visiting us, sent her a toy trumpet. Lora soon learnt to render ear-splitting blasts on this when it was held for her. Another admirer sent her a small xylophone complete with beater. She would hold the beater in her front teeth and bang any note to which I pointed. Her self-imposed practising on these various instruments drove us almost to distraction at times. It became necessary to put them out of her reach and allow her to play them only for short periods in the evenings. An unfortunate result of the singing lessons I had given her was that now, whenever Aunt or I began to play the piano, Lora, were she in the vicinity, would immediately lift her head and wail fortissimo. It is well nigh impossible to struggle through a Brahms sonata with a seal singing at the top of its voice. So most of our playing had to be done when she was in the lochan.

Pessimistic friends and relations had all predicted that our stay at the croft would be a short one. "Mind you come and see us directly you get back to civilisation," was the tone of the letters we received on arrival at the croft. When a year had passed and it became evident that we were in no hurry to return to civilisation the tone of the letters changed, and many a harried, town-dwelling friend wrote saying she envied us the peace and quiet of our lives. Peace we had certainly found, but a musical seal, two boisterous otters and other fauna do not make for the quietest of lives even in remote Sutherland.

Birds are comparatively tame up here, though not so numerous or varied in species as in the coastal areas. Among those which visited the vicinity of the croft were ring ouzels, stonechats, blackbirds, thrushes, twites, and meadow-pipits. Close by the byre grew a rowan tree and two silver birches and this tiny glade drew a number of temporary and semi-permanent bird visitors. A cuckoo was a regular visitor during the summer months. We missed its haunting, two-note song when it migrated. This bird grew so tame that it would perch on an outstretched arm and fly on to our shoulders when we were working in the garden.

However isolated the area in which one lives there is always the chance of rats eventually catching up with one, particularly when livestock is kept so that grain and fodder have to be stored. Rats were the cause of thirty people, the entire population of North Rona, starving to death on that island in 1686. They came ashore off a wreck and ate up the barley which was the inhabitants' chief food supply. When visiting the township we used to be in half a mind whether to acquire a kitten in order to ward off this possible menace. But the knowledge that a kitten would also be a deterrent to the birds decided us against getting one. Rodney apart, we were fortunate in never being troubled by rats whilst at the croft. More and more birds came to haunt our patch of land and old friends returned year after year, the cuckoo amongst them. There was one species of bird whose absence we would have welcomed, and that was the hoodie crow, perhaps the worst pest of the highlands. It does enormous damage to crops, sucks the eggs of other birds, including the grouse, thus earning the opprobrium of game-keepers, and it attempts to drive other birds away from its vicinity. Our problem was how to drive off the hoodies without scaring away the more welcome visitors. Whenever we found a maimed bird or animal, or—during the winter—one suffering from the effects of a severe spell of weather, we would bring it in and attempt to heal or revive it. Aunt Miriam was an amateur, though not inconsiderable, vet. Our first victim up here chanced to be one of these hoodies. I found it in a dip of the moors with a badly torn wing. It was put into a wire cage and its injury attended to. When it had fully recovered it was released.

For those who genuinely love birds and animals it is no easy task deciding where to draw the line between rank sentimentalism and unnecessary slaughter. The word "vermin" as used by some would include every creature which deprived mankind of the merest jot of his own foodstuffs. At the other extreme are those who say we have no right to take any creature's life and are erring when we imbibe a glass of milk—milk belonging, according to their lights, solely to the calf. But these extremists have been unforthcoming in putting forward suggestions as to how they would solve the rat and hoodie problem, among others. Animals are killed for their leather as well as for meat, but the most saintly vegetarian seems to think nothing of wearing leather shoes and carrying a leather wallet, while he is ever ready to shout with disgust—"dead flesh!"—when confronted with the meat-eating fraternity. Having written a little on what seem to me flaws in the ethics of others where bird, beast and fish are concerned, let me expose an anomaly in my own ethics, if I have not already done so. Of recent years I have brought myself to kill any creature whose malady or injuries I have felt uncertain of being able to heal reasonably quickly and painlessly, even though the act of killing invariably fills me with repulsion. I take home any ailing creature which I believe I shall be able to heal, whether it be rat or hoodie, and try to do what I can for it. Yet I would not hesitate to kill rats which invaded my premises, nor to join with those who say the numbers of certain species, including the beautiful red deer, should be kept within definite limits. Red deer can be a real menace to the croft dweller, as we were later to discover. But all killing, I believe, should be as swift and painless as possible, and those who have to kill should make sure that they use methods which are so.

A person who has the inborn quality of being able to attract wild creatures is a rarity—these days, at any rate. I have known only two people who possess this faculty, one of whom was Aunt Miriam. Her mother noticed when she was quite a small child that if she were left alone in the garden birds would hop round her and flit on to her shoulders. At the approach of anyone else they would fly off. For a long while Aunt was unaware that this attraction birds felt for her was in any way unusual. Animals were drawn to her too. She never had any fear of them. For a number of years I believed that wild creatures perhaps sensed in her a lack of the urge to kill and this partially accounted for their behaviour towards her. Later, when I met an elderly Eskimo trapper in Iceland who also had this unusual gift I was compelled to discount such a theory. I have seen this man sitting in open country with as many as five rabbits cropping the grass round him. And he was able to pick one up and fondle it as though it were a pet without the rabbit evincing the slightest alarm. Yet had he felt inclined for a rabbit supper he would not have hesitated to wring its neck. Needless to say, this man had been a highly successful trapper and had seldom lacked for meat. If he walked through a spinney of birch scrub a whistle would bring birds fluttering to him. Though he never scrupled to use his power over wild creatures to his own advantage, this Eskimo would carry a small leather pochet on his person filled with grain and bits of fat to feed the birds, which flew to him as if to a magnet. Like Aunt, he could offer no explanation as to why he should possess this rare gift except that his father had likewise possessed it, and his grandfather also. So it seems probable that it can be inherited. In Aunt Miriam's case this was not so; neither of her parents was gifted in this way. Although I did not have the good fortune to possess the gift either, I did discover a very useful means whereby I could hold the attention of wild seals—and a tame one—when I came to study them later. It also had the effect of largely dispelling their fear of my person. Man is and ever has been the seal's greatest enemy. At my school down south I had made and learnt to play a simple bamboo finger pipe. The tone was pleasant, but the range of notes only extended an octave so the number of tunes which could be played on it was limited. We had been at the croft well over a year before I troubled to unpack it. On hearing the sound of pipe music Lora— who was sitting outside shaking a tin which a thoughtful guest had filled with pebbles for her—came in, dropped the tin on the floor, and sat herself in front of me. Though I have no knowledge of seances, it appeared to me that she went into a light trance; her eyes had a far-away look and she seemed quite oblivious of everything except the music. As long as I continued to play she sat there, still and absorbed, never attempting to sing. And this was the way pipe music always affected her. Again, as with the piano, it made no impression on the other animals.

Whenever I took one of her instruments from her Lora would start a rumpus of whining and barking which could be sorely trying to the nerves. Having seen the effect piping had on her I began to use subtler methods. While Lora was going over the National Anthem for the umpteenth time on the xylophone, whacking each note with verve if not always with accuracy, I would start playing the pipe. She would glance up, the beater would drop from her mouth, and in a moment she would be spellbound, sitting quietly with her eyes half closed. Still playing, with never a let up, I would sneak away her toy and place it on a shelf. When the music stopped and she opened her eyes and gazed about her, she would look mildly surprised at finding her plaything gone but on these occasions she never whined for its return. The piping had fulfilled its purpose—for ten minutes or so at any rate.

Visitors to the croft could never understand why we would not let Lora play and sing, for hours on end, which she would have been perfectly happy to do if given the chance. Although they would tell us in their letters that they were looking forward immensely to the quiet of the wilderness, the rude shattering of this quiet by Lora in one of her recitals did not appear to worry them in the least. On the contrary, they enjoyed every minute of them and were as disappointed as she was when they were brought to an abrupt close by Aunt or myself. But a week of listening to Lora running through her repertoire was not the same thing as hearing it month after month and eventually, year after year.

After a time we were forced to the rather humiliating conclusion that friends came on visits mainly to get acquainted with Lora; our company, peace and quiet, the beauties of the countryside were little more than sidelights.

"Where is she?" a guest would ask, the moment he had dumped down his suitcase and gulped a cup of tea to revive himself after the rigours of the journey.

"Out in the lochan."

The guest would take a quick look at the rolling sea of hills, rocks and pockets of water stretching in every direction to the far horizon, and then—"Well ... can't she be got in?"

We would stroll down to the lochan, the guest carrying the trumpet in readiness, and we would stare across the sheet of water, devoid of any sign of animal life. I would call and presently we would see the small, dark speck of her head coming towards us, with perhaps a smaller one nearby belonging to an otter. In less than a minute she would be ashore and, the trumpet pressed against her mouth, giving a rendering of 'Danny Boy'. Her boisterous good nature and love of showing off before visitors made her ever ready to play. A certain uncle of mine took a great fancy to her. At his home outside Aberdeen he used to hold monthly ceilidhs (musical evenings) at which local talent used to perform. Uncle Andrew became obsessed with the idea that Lora should be a guest at one of these ceilidhs. He felt sure his musical friends would appreciate her gifts and delight in a performance from her. Ever one to make light of difficulties, he assured Aunt Miriam that the lengthy journey to Aberdeen with a seal could be easily accomplished. Shortly after he had visited us he arrived one evening in his brake to collect Lora and me. We set off early the following morning. I had packed two suitcases, one containing my belongings, the other Lora's instruments and her mackintosh. Uncle informed me that he had got in a large supply of fish, biscuits and oil. When he had left home his wife had been busy catching the goldfish in their pond and putting them into a wooden rain butt. Any that refused to be caught would have to take a chance with Lora. The pond was hers for the duration of our visit. As Uncle had predicted, the journey was accomplished without mishap. The brake bounced over the track and several times came perilously near to sliding down a hillside. Lora took the bumps and jolts calmly and appeared to enjoy the ride.

On the evening of the ceilidh I led her into the drawing room where it was to be held. My feelings about the forthcoming proceedings were dubious. A well known singer of mouth music (unaccompanied singing) was coming and had consented to start the evening with a song. A melodeon player was to take the platform next, followed by Lora giving an exhibition of xylophone playing. That was to comprise the first half of the evening.

There would be a break for supper. During the second half, amongst other attractions, Lora was to sing to my piano accompaniment. So far so good.

The guests started to arrive. Lora, the most sociable and

extroverted of creatures, greeted them warmly. I suggested to Uncle, as the first artist took her place at the far end of the room, that I should shut Lora into his study until it was her turn to perform. But he and several of the guests vetoed this suggestion at once. She must stay. The singer smiled charmingly and started off with the assurance of a professional. She managed to sing a few notes of an old Hebridean air before the inevitable happened; Lora raised her head and roared her way from a deep bass to a seal top C. Even a full Covent Garden chorus would not have been able to compete with that, and the singer wisely gave up there and then. The audience were hysterical with laughter. They had not heard anything as good as that for a long while. When a certain amount of calm had been restored someone suggested that Lora be allowed to perform first and the human faction later; thus she would get her little act off her chest and be willing to listen to others. It was blatantly apparent that he had no knowledge of seals whatsoever, but by then she was out of my hands and being stage-managed by others. She was lifted bodily on to the top of the piano by two stalwart males so that the audience would get a good view of her, and the xylophone was placed before her. I stood by her side ready to point to the notes in case she should be overcome by a sudden fit of nerves at the sight of so large an audience and momentarily forget her piece. My presence proved unnecessary. She took the beater from me and started off with aplomb on 'Baa-baa Black Sheep'. The audience strained forward. I caught murmurs of—"Yes, I recognised that bit."

"Quite incredible…" and "Isn't she playing 'Danny Boy' now?"

"No, I'm sure she isn't. Oh, perhaps she might be…"

Loud applause greeted the final slither of the beater along

the length of the instrument which denoted the end of 'Danny Boy' and was followed by vociferous calls for an encore.

"Carry on," said Uncle, beaming at me.

I thought the front row, consisting of the other prospective performers looked a trifle discouraged at the way things were going. I announced 'Where my Caravan has Rested'.

"I used to sing that as a subaltern in the First World War," a charming grey-haired gentleman confessed to the room at large. "My wife always—"

We never heard what. Lora got off to a speedy start, whacking notes left, right and centre. The caravan had apparently got loose from its moorings and was rushing towards a head-on collision. There was a loud crash as the xylophone fell to the floor, pushed off by Lora's exuberant playing. The audience rose to its feet. After a short pause in which to recover their breath, people uttered more fulsome exclamations of delight: "Marvellous, isn't she?"

"Yes, brilliant. I didn't happen to know the tune myself but I'm sure she played it superbly—encore!"

The turn ended somewhat more soberly with a rendering of the National Anthem. The melodeon player got up. He did not appear too happy at having to follow such a popular performer. I began to realise why professional actors so heartily dislike children and animals taking part in a play; when they are around nobody else gets a look in. His misgivings proved to be correct. He failed as lamentably to make an impression in competition with the loudly singing Lora as had the first performer. With great good humour he walked back to his seat defeated and Lora again took the platform, this time to play the mouth organ.

After supper I made up my mind to take things in hand a little. For my part, I very much wanted to hear the melodeon player in action, but if the second half of the evening followed the trend of the first that pleasure seemed unlikely to be ful-filled. While the rest were busy eating and talking I managed to enveigle Lora into Uncle Andrew's study and close the door on her. The study most unfortunately was not soundproof and when the music started her piteous wails at being excluded from the proceedings drew the attention of the guests. Someone went along at once to let her out.

In a final attempt to keep order I made her sit by my side and told her severely to be quiet. The result was no less disastrous. Seals have free-flowing tear ducts and the patch of skin im-mediately below the eyes is continually moist. Lora, overcome with frustration at not being allowed to take part, sat with tears pouring down her face. Whereupon the sympathetic guests pleaded on her behalf and the other performers generously allowed her to take the platform yet again. The evening finished with a singsong in which, I need hardly say, Lora outsang the rest of us. But I was assured by Uncle that the ceilidh had been a great success.

on land and water

The country up here is uncluttered by housing and lofty vegetation. At first one misses the woods and the green lushness
of field and hedgerow, and one even longs at times for such
homely sights as an errand boy swinging down a street on his
bicycle or a display of wares in a grocer's. But very soon the
wilderness begins to exert its fascination, and its grip on one
tightens relentlessly as the weeks go by. This countryside, one
feels, is quite indifferent to Man. It is not 'pretty', not softened
in the least by a touch of civilisation. Roads may curl through
the valleys and, in certain districts, telegraph poles stand like
lopped trees against a horizon, but these man-made things
only serve to emphasise if anything the vastness and pristine
wildness of the land. Sky, hill, loch, burn; burn, loch, hill and
sky—this is the major theme which the eye notes. There are
minor ones as well. The grass, short and tough, is of a grey-
ish-green colour, almost a dull blue in certain lights, and it is
interspersed with clumps of heather. Heather does not grow in
any profusion up here. Many of the summits of the higher hills
are virtually devoid of vegetation. Some are covered with loose
scree which makes walking difficult and tiring. The sounds
are of water flowing down the hillsides, rain, wind, the cries of

birds and beasts. On a hot day when a fair distance from the croft I would sometimes hear the clink of the spade hitting a stone as Aunt Miriam dug in the garden, or her voice calling an animal. Except for a few intermittent sounds such as these, and the sight of the croft lying encircled by hills, there was nothing else to bring to mind humanity and its doings.

I once heard a surveyor, who had travelled much in deserts, say how disappointed he had felt on seeing his first oasis. He had driven out to it from a town over miles of sand and all he saw when he got there were a few unexceptional palms and a pool of dirty water surrounded by thick mud. His second oasis affected him differently. He reached it after weeks of gruelling travel in the Sahara. Throughout those weeks the only shade to be had during the day was under cover of their small tent. Except for an occasional thorn bush there was never a glimpse of a tree, only the monotonous sand dunes rolling endlessly into space. Water was rationed to half a pint a day and when they were approaching the oasis they had drunk the last drop. The sight of the green palms in the distance seemed to him almost miraculous, as later did the moist earth and taste of water. Never again, he vowed, would he take the sight of greenery, cool shade and water for granted. That is the correct way, of course, to approach an oasis.

I have recounted this little tale because—in a less drastic fashion perhaps—it conjures up for me a certain aspect of Sutherland. Here one learns to appreciate what, in less exigent parts, one almost takes for granted. One's eyesight sharpens too. One's hearing becomes keener. And from this barren land one never ceases to pluck strangely rewarding experiences.

We had been at the croft two years and I believed that I knew the country within a mile's radius fairly well. As I was walking over the hills one day quite close to home I chanced to find myself going down an incline, at the bottom of which was a thick tangle of birch scrub. I could not remember having seen it before. Pushing my way through the birches and undergrowth I found myself facing a tiny lochan. Birds flew upwards or scuttled to a hide in the reeds. Floating on the brown peat water were the white heads of water lilies. Since then I have seen great lakes covered in a profusion of these flowers but none has given me more pleasure than this lochan—hardly bigger than a good sized round table—hidden in a dip of the austere Sutherland hills.

Throughout the seven years we lived here I saw few strangers and these were all tinkers; no hiker, sportsman or tourist. The people we saw were the friends who visited us, and the postman, the shepherd, Mr. McNairn, and the Frasers, an old crofting couple who were our next nearest neighbours after him. They lived six miles distant.

Much has yet to be learnt about the movement of seals under the water and the length of time they can remain submerged. When Lora was in the lochan I took to going out in the rowboat, a stopwatch in my hand. The length of her dives varied from a few seconds to several minutes. The longest dive I timed lasted over sixteen minutes. She was then in her fourth year. Grey seals have been known to submerge for twenty-two minutes and the great elephant seal, whose domain is the southern seas, for thirty-five, but it seems possible that longer dives for all species have yet to be recorded. Since a seal's ears and nostrils are closed while under water, it is believed by some that seals find their food mainly by sight. I myself am a little doubtful of this.

We took Lora in a friend's car to the mouth of a tidal river. The estuary was not deep. The water was very muddy and discoloured. While we ate our sandwiches, Lora went swimming, and after a dive lasting less than a minute surfaced with a fish dangling from her mouth. During the course of the afternoon she caught several others. Perhaps seals use their whiskers to aid or replace eyesight on occasion. It was three years later that we motored again to within a mile of this spot. Here we sat on the beach while Lora swam in the sea. When the time came to go home she was not to be seen. Repeated calls brought no result. Anyone who has spent weary minutes calling a reluctant dog from a wood will understand how aggravating this can be. With a seal last seen sporting in the waves there is the added frustration of not being able to go and investigate the whereabouts of the truant. At the end of an hour of calling and scanning the ocean, all to no purpose, I remembered the estuary and suggested, without much hope, that we go and look for her there. It was always a worry when she disappeared as seals make an easy target for a man with a gun. There was no sign of her when we reached the mouth but I called her name and she soon appeared on the opposite side of the bank and swam across to us, having, no doubt, done a little fishing in the meantime. This incident is curious. During the previous visit she had swum only a few yards into the open sea and could not possibly have seen the beach we had just left, as it was round an escarpment of rock, yet some sure instinct had connected the two places and had taken her back to the fishing territory again.

There was a rock about twelve feet in height which overhung the lochan where the water was deep. Lora used to enjoy diving off it. After a time, possibly under her influence, the otters came to enjoy this sport too, flinging their long, supple bodies from it in the most carefree manner and trying to push one another off in a general rough-house. Both wild seals and otters are animals which enjoy playing games. They have their own traditional ones. Otters in all parts of the world make mud chutes on river banks and slide down them, landing with a splash in the water. During winter they make snow chutes, not necessarily by water, and kicking off with their hind feet, their forepaws doubled under by their sides, they slide down as swiftly as a toboggan. This game Lora came to learn from the otters. Otters are swift and strong swimmers but they have not the speed of a seal. When any water game was in progress Lora used to be an easy winner. It was a sad sight to watch the persevering Ben doing his best to keep pace with these three expert swimmers. They knew his limited capacities in the water. Many a time I have seen Lora or an otter with the ball in their mouths glance behind to make sure that Ben was following up in the faint hope of seizing it. They would deliberately slow down and when he was within a short distance of them, dive below the surface and reappear a little later in another spot. This always got Ben barking with exasperation. I used to wonder why he persisted in joining in the water games when he had such a thin time of it. Besides having a rowboat, I later became the proud possessor of a collapsible canvas canoe with a double paddle. I could get up a good speed in this, but never became swift enough to beat Lora or the otters when starting even. Seals and otters are quick to learn and ever eager to take part in a game, so I devised a water race. They would remain on the shore or rock until I shouted the word "Go!" having in the interval given myself a generous start. A series of splashes to the rear would assure me that my adversaries had dived from the rock and were after me. I would paddle furiously, but I have to confess that in spite of my initial advantage I seldom won a race. While a race was in progress there would be no sound except for the dip of the paddle in the water and an occasional bark from the rather highly strung Gretel. But no sooner had they clambered ashore at the far end of the lochan than they would start to bark excitedly. To me, there was something faintly sinister in the way my adversaries silently bore down on me. On these occasions Lora seldom raised her head as she did when swimming more leisurely. Her body, just breaking the surface of the water, was like a dark torpedo. The actual colour of a Common Seal's coat is a greenish amber, scattered liberally over the upper parts with brownish-black spots. Like all seals, she took pleasure in swimming on her back in leisure moments—as did the otters—sometimes holding the ball between her front, flipper-like paws. Both she and the otters could reverse in the water as easily and rapidly as a fish. Their bodies when swimming appeared to be boneless.

I was out in the lochan one day with a full boat load comprising Lora, the otters and Ben, when I received one of my periodic duckings. The cause of it was a deer. Ben started to yelp furiously and then dived over the side of the boat. I just caught sight of the deer's black nose and its antlers, parallel to the water, which was all that could be seen of it. The boat gave a tremendous lurch as Lora and the otters followed Ben's lead, and I found myself in the water. I managed to right the boat and collect the oars before clambering back into it. The noise and commotion were shocking. Seal and otters had caught up with the deer and were snapping and diving about it. I was afraid that it would use its antlers on them if they did not keep their distance, though this doubtless would have been difficult for it to do to any purpose while out of its depth. It swum on relentlessly. At one point it and Lora were swimming side by side, Lora undecided, apparently, as to how she should act. When it sprang to the shore it gave itself a brief shake and then galloped away towards the hills. It was a magnificent stag with all its rights (a full head of antlers). Ben next took up the chase. Having made land, he scampered after it in full cry like a trained deerhound. Long after he had disappeared his shrill barking came back to me from somewhere in the hills. He did not return till late that evening, worn out with the chase and too weary to touch any food. Since that day he frequently took himself off to the hills, sometimes from early morning till late evening, and was always so tired when he returned home that he would just flop down and go straight to sleep. If it was not in reality already too late to do so, it seems to me now that it was then we should have taken him firmly in hand. But we never thought to do so, letting him find his pleasures where he would, free to come and go like the rest of the animals.

Looking through the notebook I kept for that year I find two events which I considered worthy to be underlined in red ink.

"July 20th—The arrival of Sith (reads one of these entries, and goes on)*: "The most delicate, beautiful creature I have ever seen. His coat is a dark red dotted with white spots. These will disappear as he grows older. Long, flexible ears edged with black hair. Have not measured him yet but should say he stands at about thirty-eight inches. Orphan. Brought over from the Reay Forest. (Another surprise gift from a friend of a friend of Mr. McNairn's). Five weeks old. Spent most of the evening trying to think of a name which would convey delicacy and speed. Finally decided on Sith (This is Gaelic for fairy). Has the byre to himself at the moment as the goats and pony sleep out during the summer."*

This creature, whom on arrival I considered to be a veritable gift of the gods, was a roe buck calf. Nothing is more delightful than to watch one of these exquisitely formed little creatures as it leaps into the air and springs effortlessly on to any hillock lying in its path. But the temperaments of these creatures leave much to be desired, as I was later to discover.

It is probable that while one person may succeed in training one kind of animal, another may have better success with a different species. I have heard it said that otters are impossible to train and will always remain intractable and liable to bite the hand of the loving owner. I have not found this to be so. I have never expected perfection from any creature and consider they have a right to an occasional day of bad temper just as we have. But I searched vainly for one admirable trait in Sith's character. Like all our animals, he was reared without ever being given a slap or touch of the stick; all training was done by voice and gesture. At first we were amused by his predilection for butting every living thing which came within his orbit, including ourselves. But as the sharp little horns started to grow we began to find his playfulness—as we had first termed his delight in butting—not quite so amusing. Vainly I would order him in severe tones to desist. It was useless. Nor did he hesitate to use his excellent set of teeth—I, $^0/_3$. C, $^0/_0$. PM, $^3/_3$. M, $^3/_3$. by two, equals thirty—as the dental formula goes, to good purpose. He had no desire to nuzzle the outstretched hand. All he wanted, and quick, was that bit of carrot or apple. If the hand did not proffer the expected titbit then it received a hard bite. It was no use protesting inwardly, as I used to, that having gone to considerable trouble to rear him I was entitled to a little friendly affection. I myself have been quite unsuccessful in training deer. In my opinion they have cold temperaments, are impossible to train and are always liable to bite the hand of the loving owner. That the owner should get butted too, goes without saying. Sith, the fairy, did not turn out to be quite the gentle, affectionate creature I had believed him to be on first acquaintance.

The other animals too, not without cause, found his presence irksome in the extreme. Most of them had their favourite resting places. Ben's was the wall round the garden. Here he would lie for hours, sleeping, watching all that was going on in the lochan below, now and then reversing his position so as to be able to see what was taking place around the croft. Sith found it easy enough while still a youngster to spring on to the wall. And though still a youngster it was apparent he possessed remarkable strength for his size. With a well aimed butt he sent Ben flying off the wall with a surprised yelp. It was not to be the only occasion that Ben was the victim of such an experience.

An atmosphere of apprehension prevailed when Sith was around. One day I discovered the gallant little Rodney being ruthlessly butted against an outer wall of the croft. Rats are most courageous creatures. With every man's hand against them, they have to be in order to survive. Though firmly pinioned and with much of the air knocked out of him, he still managed to squeak with fury and struggled to free himself. The space between Sith's horns then was not much more than two-and-a-half inches, but, by great good fortune, with each butt the horns landed either side of Rodney. I shudder to think of his fate if it had been otherwise. No sooner had I released him than he went for Sith's hind legs, Sith meanwhile having turned his attention to me. A sharp bite from the incensed Rodney sent him flying off along the track with a grace which always held me spellbound.

I am glad to say that Sith eventually took himself off. But we had not seen the last of him.

I awoke suddenly one night to find the light of a full moon streaming into the room. It was not the moon shining on my face which had awakened me but the sound of a lettuce being

seal morning

uprooted and munched. Hurriedly flinging off the covers, I crossed the room and looked out. A charming sight to all but a crofter met my gaze. The sky was a vivid, mysterious blue. Under the round white disc of the moon lay the darker blue hills and the black rocks. The water of the lochan shone black and silver. Nearby in the garden every plant was clearly silhouetted and touched with a film of blue. So was the sylphlike roe buck methodically wrenching up the lettuces. I climbed out of the window, not stopping to put on my slippers, and walked over the earth in my bare feet. Sith came high-stepping towards me and promptly landed a butt on my legs which were covered only by a flimsy cotton nightdress. My cry of anguish woke all the inhabitants of the croft. Sith made a leisurely getaway over the wall.

"Have you been sleep walking?" Aunt Miriam asked, seeing me standing there in the middle of the vegetable patch.

"Sith!" I moaned, hobbling into the parlour.

A lamp was lit to throw more light on the scene. It was revealed that my left leg was streaming with blood from a gash just below the knee joint. The gash was not very wide but it was a good deep one. Aunt Miriam threaded a needle with white silk and dipped silk and needle into a pan of boiling water. Then she proceeded to sew me up. My moonlight encounter with my late pet had cost me three stitches. Found to be missing the following morning was one row of lettuce.

For those who are romantically minded, let me add that Sith returned once more to his old home, this time accompanied by a doe. The pair of them leapt on to the wall but were promptly seen off by Aunt before they did any damage.

The other event which I underlined in red concerned a thrush. The song-thrush is sometimes called a mavis in Scotland. This thrush, a cock, was one of the tamest of our

44

bird visitors. He never left the vicinity of the croft for long. Whenever there was a spell of severe weather we would put out food for the birds each day and hang a large straw-filled box on the lea of the croft. The box was built entirely of wood and the entrance was by way of a round hole at one side. Thus it afforded the maximum of protection from wind and cold. Breac (speckled), as we called him, used to take advantage of these amenities. If a window of the croft was open he would fly in and perch on a picture rail, out of reach of the animals. Should one of us call him he would fly down on to a hand or shoulder. His singing was above thrush average. Almost every morning when the weather was mild he used to fly into Aunt's bedroom around six o'clock, perch on the bed rail and utter clear piping notes until Aunt roused herself and spoke a few words to him. Then he would hop about the room and take a drink from the enamel water can. That March—a little later than thrushes farther south—he and his mate started to build a nest in the rowan. We watched the proceedings with interest, hoping that no hen cuckoo would arrive on the scene with a view to laying her egg in the nest. These birds do not as a rule choose thrushes nests in which to deposit their eggs, prefer-ring the nests of smaller birds, but it has not been unknown for them to do so. Throughout the day Breac dutifully fed his mate as she sat on the eggs, going backwards and forwards to the rowan tree. He was far too busy now to come into the croft, though he would spend a minute on our shoulders occasionally if we were in the open. When the four young were hatched the tempo of his working day increased. Like most birds during the nesting season, he lost weight and his appearance, previously sleek and trim, began to look rather bedraggled. Human beings are not the only ones who like to have their offspring admired. As we were having breakfast one

45

morning there was a tap on the window and looking towards it, we saw the whole thrush family lined up on the sill.

These youngsters became as tame as their parents and all attained maturity. A limit had to be drawn somewhere. When a fledgeling hopped inside I would place it on a finger and put it out again. Aunt found the early morning situation rather more difficult to deal with, for now Breac and his whole family would arrive and line up on the bed rail, the fledgelings cheeping loudly.

A bird whose numbers is slowly increasing round these parts is the raven. Not many years ago there was a possibility of it becoming extinct in Britain owing to the depredations of bird nesters and its destruction at the hands of gamekeepers. It does take a toll of game and lambs, but its main food is carrion and the smaller mammals such as rats and mice. Its favourite nesting places are tall elms and lofty crags. Nowadays bird nesting is slowly going out of fashion, people instructing their children to leave eggs in the nest so as later to have the pleasure of watching the young birds. But thirty and forty years ago people took delight in potting at ravens and robbing their nests. Storming a raven's nest was considered to be an act of great daring and skill, hence it was often undertaken by energetic climbers, young and not so young. I will quote an account of one such venture as described by a Mr. Capper, who made the perilous ascent near Earls Colne.

"The nest was at the top of an immense elm," he writes, "which stood on a little clearing in a copse. The hen slipped off the moment we emerged from the undergrowth and we did not see her again; but the cock instantly flew down towards us with a menacing bark to give battle. We were well acquainted with his complacent 'pruk! pruk!' as he used to sail over the valley in his daily rambles; but this was an angry, hoarse growl.

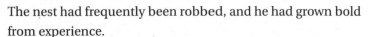

The nest had frequently been robbed, and he had grown bold from experience.

"We were soon at the foot of the tree, and, throwing a line over the lowest available bough, were in a position whence we could ascend farther, aided by our hands and feet. The nest was at an immense height. As we drew nearer to it the raven became bolder, and we had to stop occasionally to menace him. At times he must have been within a few yards of us, sailing from one tree to another, and darting at us as he passed. At last we reached the nest—a large structure of twigs of many years' accumulation, very compact and difficult to reach round. It was built almost at the top of the tree, in a fork at the end of a bough, and in a position not very safe to hold on by. With care, cap between our teeth to keep our friend off, we got one hand over the nest and could just balance ourselves sufficiently to look over its edge. There, to our delight, on the lining of sheeps' wool and fine fibre, rather deep down, lay three fresh eggs... By great care and by keeping the bird at bay with our handkerchief we succeeded in getting them safely down. We slowly retired as we came, the cock bird tearing off twigs and driving us before him, with ruffled feathers, savage barks, and short menacing sallies; and it was not until we were at some distance from his nesting-place that we really felt out of danger..."

Such dare-devilry does not often take place these days, fortunately for the raven. I was once offered a young raven but refused the gift on account of Rodney and the squirrels, thus missing a chance to study close at hand this interesting and intelligent bird. The lives of Rodney and the squirrels were in constant peril owing to the number of birds of prey which dwell in these parts. Their habit of sitting on the roof added to their peril but there was nothing we could do to protect them short of shutting them up in cages, a penalty we had no intention of submitting them to. Better a short life and a gay one than a dreary one in a cage. As things turned out, Cuthbert's life was a short one. He was snatched off the roof one day in the claws of a peregrine falcon.

croft life in summer

Among the jobs we had to get through during summer were digging, drying, and stacking peat; scything grass for hay and stooking it; picking berries—raspberries, wild strawberries; blaeberries, sloes—for bottling, jam and wine-making. We dried herbs, mushrooms, and edible fungi. Repairs to croft and byre were carried out during warm weather. Every fortnight we made a trip to the township in the pony trap to collect supplies. A certain number of tins of food and fuel and items of clothing would be stored at once against the following winter. We worked long hours in the garden. It became too small for our needs and so we made another one on a patch of ground near the lochan where the soil was richer. With these two gardens, devoted solely to the cultivation of vegetables, our supply of fresh green food during the summer months was assured.

When living in remote parts it is necessary to know how to deal with minor accidents and illnesses, and to have a basic knowledge of diet, so that one can plan well-balanced and healthy meals. Throughout our years at the croft we did not suffer a single illness and kept clear of even slight colds. Tinned and dehydrated foods were used only in an emergency during summer and as a supplementary food supply during winter. Cakes and bread were made from brown flour. Besides the homegrown vegetables, we also made good use of wild green-stuffs.

With a base of lettuce leaves, grated carrot and goats' milk cheese we concocted some excellent salads, using such herbage as sorrel leaves, watercress, which grew in abundance in certain streams, and dandelion leaves. Several dandelion plants grew in the croft garden and these, unlike the ones in our garden down south which had been ruthlessly dug up, were encouraged to grow and flourish.

Out on a walk we discovered a ruined shieling. In the old days people used to bring their cows and goats to the high hills during summer so that the animals could crop the rich grass. Up in these high pasture lands they lived in simple stone and thatched dwellings called shielings. This practice of bringing cattle to higher ground for part of the year has largely died out and consequently the ground round croft dwellings is badly overcropped.

The roof of this shieling had long since caved in and there was only one wall still standing. Almost equalling it in height was a profusion of nettles. They proved a welcome food supply and we ate them from early spring to late autumn. They were nicest during spring when the young tops were very tender. I would walk up to the shieling wearing a pair of leather gloves and carrying a basket. Having filled the basket with nettles, I would strip the stems from the older leaves. They were cooked like spinach; well pressed down in a pan which had been filled with a very small amount of salted water, and then boiled over a low fire for ten to fifteen minutes. When cooked properly nettles should require no draining. They were turned into a heated dish and dabs of butter were added. The flavour was delicious. For a supper dish we used to top the nettles with a poached egg; for lunch we would grate a little cheese over them to add variety or, if we had been lucky with our tomatoes, souse them in tomato sauce. In all, we devised nine different ways of serving nettles.

When both goats were in milk there was more than sufficient for our needs and the surplus was converted into cheese. Having curdled, it was turned into a linen square which was strung up from a branch of the rowan. When the whey had dripped off, salt and pepper were added to the curds and sometimes a few chopped herbs. The result was goats' milk cottage cheese.

We took it in turns to milk the goats. During summer we rose early, six or six-thirty, and while one was setting the breakfast table the other would be on the milking stool. The goats slept in the open and were milked outside in the warmer weather. Each day they would be restaked on a fresh patch of turf. Rodney took to coming and sitting beside me while I milked and every so often, if I were in a magnanimous mood, I would squirt a jet of the liquid in his direction. He would lick the drops from his face and wait hopefully for another sousing. These actions of mine on Rodney's behalf proved to be a mistake for we later caught him several times helping himself from a teat while the goat—making no attempt to rid herself of him—rested on the ground. I do not know how he managed to extract the milk without hurting the goat, for rats have sharp teeth. Once he had acquired this habit we had great difficulty in breaking him of it.

First to be up and about in the mornings were the otters who would take themselves down to the lochan for a swim. As they grew older we often did not see them again till the evening when they returned for their supper of bread-and-mash. Next to rise would be the squirrels.

After Cuthbert's sudden departure, Sara took to sleeping with Rodney in his box. There was no moaning at the bar for her lost mate where she was concerned. After he left she became better tempered and more amenable. There had always been considerable competition between Cuthbert and Rodney for her attentions. Presumably Rodney, as there was no female rat around, looked to Sara for companionship. This did not put him in favour with Cuthbert. Furious chitterings and squeaks would come from the vicinity of the roof and then we would know that the two males were at it again. Sara would come pelting in at the door, chirruping with agitation, and climb hastily into her wicker basket, but before long the two rivals would be hurrying along after her.

It was interesting to note the various moves and sounds which this male rat made in order to lure the female squirrel into his box. Perhaps Cuthbert would be in the basket, Rodney in his box and Sara on the carpet or perched on a ledge of the dresser. A soft chitter from Cuthbert would inform her that her presence was required in the basket. She would start towards it and then, to her bewilderment, would come a low, drawn-out squeak from the box by the dresser; a very different sort of squeak from the kind Cuthbert was treated to. Sara would turn, undecided. Another low, come-hither squeak, and the sight of Rodney sitting up in his box would have her hurrying to him. Then there would come a more commanding chitter from the basket and perhaps Cuthbert would emerge, his tail flickering. If Sara should happen to enter the box he would leap from the basket on to a chair, spring down and streak across the carpet. In order to avoid quite an unpleasant little set-to I would pick Sara up and put her in the basket. It was not to be wondered at that her temper sometimes became frayed under these trying circumstances. Tension relaxed after Cuthbert went. The basket was removed from the hook and henceforth she and Rodney shared the box between them.

It used to amuse me to watch Rodney—never much of a one for being stroked by Aunt or myself, though he liked to curl up on our laps in the evenings—sitting still for minutes at a time while Sara went over his coat. Rats, incidentally, are most cleanly creatures. When living away from drains and refuse they are not dirty or verminous. Rodney spent a lot of time each day washing his face, nibbling his fur, going over his tail, whiskers and ears. To reach the various parts of his anatomy he would contort his body to a surprising degree. When it came to cleaning the patch behind his ears he would lick a paw thoroughly, like a cat, and then sweep it behind and over the ear. After Sara had finished his grooming to her satisfaction she would sit with her head cocked to one side and Rodney learnt to know that this attitude of hers meant that she expected her coat to receive attention. He would nibble away industriously at the thick fur, so long in comparison to his own.

If we had been living within range of a high tree or two Rodney would never have been able to keep pace with his companion as she leaped from branch to twig. As things were, there was nothing in the vicinity excepting the dresser which he was able to climb almost as well as she could.

For those who have never kept a rat it may come as a surprise to learn that Rodney had his admirers as well as Lora. He had a way with him, as the few discovered who were intrepid enough to allow him anywhere near them. An elderly lady used to send him a packet of nuts and raisins at regular intervals, and at Christmas he would receive as an extra two small felt bails, one of which had a string attached. The ball with the string was drawn over the ground for him to pursue and I would throw the other one short distances for him to scamper after. He enjoyed simple games like these.

We took care to note and remember the places where various edible plants and berry-bearing bushes grew. One spring Aunt Miriam discovered two sloe bushes growing in a thicket at the side of a loch. We returned there in autumn to collect the berries. That and every following year we made several bottles of sloe wine. The wild raspberry patch was also close by a loch and most seasons we picked about five pounds of berries for making jam. The fruit was also eaten fresh and baked in tarts. We always tried to have some thirty pounds of jam bottled by early September. A pound jar between us lasted a week, and at that rate of consumption thirty pounds saw us through from mid-September to April. We never had visitors to stay during winter and so were able to reckon the various quantities of food required then to a fairly narrow margin. I enjoyed the time spent in jam making and undertook myself the job of skimming off the scum. With a long wooden spoon I removed the sugary fruit scum as it rose in the pans, and swallowed it with relish after it had cooled off a bit.

Mushrooms and edible fungi did not grow in any profusion in these parts but there were a few spots where we sometimes found enough to fill a basket. An always welcome find was a young, white fleshed puffball. It was cut into slices of approximately half an inch thickness, the slices dipped into a rich egg batter and fried. They tasted excellent.

It was even more rewarding than the discovery of sloe tree or puffball to find such flowers as wild hyacinth and lily of the valley on a lower slope. When walking in the high hills we generally went together and carried a compass in case we lost our bearings should a mist suddenly descend. Here, sometimes growing a few inches below the snowline, we were occasionally

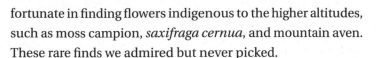

fortunate in finding flowers indigenous to the higher altitudes, such as moss campion, *saxifraga cernua*, and mountain aven. These rare finds we admired but never picked.

It was necessary to move with stealth up here if one wanted to get a close view of the red deer which grazed these high pastures.

A particular day in these hills stands out in my memory. Against previous instructions from Aunt Miriam, I had walked higher than was prudent when alone. But it was mid-June, the sky was a brilliant, translucent blue, larks sang into the breeze and the walking was good. A mountain hare gave me a sharp glance as I passed, then continued with its feeding. Now and then I heard the curious dry croak of a ptarmigan—a bird of the tops. The day gave every indication of being a propitious one for observing wild life. I had left Strath na Seilga (valley of the river Seilga) and was climbing in the direction of Creag Mhor. The azure loch, Gorm Loch Mor as it is called in Gaelic, lay to my right. Stopping a moment to survey the countryside below me, I saw to my annoyance that I was being followed by Ben. He had attempted to follow me when I left the croft, but I had ordered him home and walked forward, unrelenting. A dog is a troublesome companion when one is wanting to observe wild life for it chases and scares every creature away. I waited for the miscreant to catch me up. He encircled me and went on ahead, his nose to the ground, in the guilty fashion of a dog who is fully aware that he has disobeyed orders. I called him to me sharply and fixed a leather belt I had been wearing around his neck. His activities curtailed somewhat, we continued upwards.

Not long after Ben had made his unwelcome appearance he started to strain hard on the improvised lead. I managed to pull him up just in time. Less than a foot from him I saw to my surprise and delight a nest of young ptarmigan. It was not a nest in the usual meaning of the word, for the birds lay in a shallow hollow of the ground. Their sandy and grey plumage made them almost indistinguishable from the surrounding earth and stones. Having dragged the excited Ben over to a rock and fastened him to a convenient projection, I returned to the birds. It was the first—and last—time I discovered ptarmigan nestlings. Once again disregarding Aunt's instructions, namely, on no account to touch nestlings, let alone remove one, I extracted a handkerchief from a sleeve and kneeling down, inserted a hand among the warm, apparently fearless brood of seven. Carefully I lifted one out and placed it on the handkerchief, tying the square of linen in such a way that only the tiny head and tail were visible. To make doubly sure that it did not escape or weary itself with trying to do so, I tied a wide piece of grass round the middle of the little bundle to keep the wings tight to its sides. Then I went back for the yapping Ben. In the distance I had spotted a herd of hinds with their calves but his yapping had effectually caused them to move out of sight. I decided to make for home. Walking along a narrow corrie, the lead in one hand and the ptarmigan in the other, I began to wonder, my conscience pricking me considerably by now, whether to tell Aunt that I had just happened upon the bird lying by itself. A truthful account of how I had come by it would, I knew, earn me a severe reprimand.

A change had come over the sky since I had last taken note of it; the blue was not so intense and thin, vaporous clouds were forming. Down a cleft of the corrie blew a long streamer of mist. The sight of it made me double my pace. I remembered then that I had come without a compass as I had not planned when setting out to go so high or so far. More and more clouds were forming in the sky and puffs of mist, less vaporous now, blew with increasing frequency into the corrie. There was always the possibility that a mist would disperse as suddenly as it had come; on the other hand, it was equally possible for it to last hours or even days. I started to run, not as yet from any sense of panic, but because I realised it was imperative to reach the end of the corrie quickly and get a good view of my bearings. I was about five miles from home, high up in the hills. But it is not mileage that makes for distance and remoteness in these parts; it is the rough going, the variability of the weather conditions, and the danger of bogs and exposure. Besides the compass, we also took with us when walking in the hills a jersey and windproof jacket each to obviate the risk of exposure should the weather turn cold, and we kept in reserve a sandwich and bar of chocolate. All these things I had neglected to do, and I began to hope fervently that the floating veils of mist would prove a false alarm. I stood on the open hillside and noted the River Skinsdale far off in the valley below, the croft to the right, and a great boulder lying at the bottom of the hill which I would have to make sure of passing on my left, from there bearing steadily in a southerly direction, avoiding three large areas of bogland. There was no path to follow the whole of the way. As I started down the hill, keeping my eyes on the boulder—my immediate destination—and trying at the same time to avoid rocks and loose scree, the mist swept over the brow of the hill and enveloped me, blotting out every landmark and object excepting those within a few feet.

These mountain mists are as dense as a London pea-souper, but unlike the latter's dirty yellow colouring are as white as intangible cottonwool. If caught in one and uncertain of one's bearings, by far the best plan is to take what shelter one can find, pull on sweater and wind jacket, and stick it out, telling oneself that one still has a bar of chocolate and a sandwich to ward off the pangs of hunger. The situation can be accepted calmly under these conditions. Apart from getting chilled and a little hungry and thirsty, the hill walker should be none the worse for his experience. But if one has been foolhardy enough to come without the minimum necessities for hill walking, as I had that day, a mist can be a very real danger. I was clad in a cotton dress, had no extra clothing to put on, and had eaten all the sandwiches. Stumbling and tripping down the hill, I managed by some miracle to reach my first objective, the boulder. Here I halted and reviewed the situation. Should I remain where I was on safe ground while the mist lasted, and run the risk of exposure should it fail to lift for some hours, or should I continue forward and thereby run the equal risk of losing my sense of direction and stepping into a bog? I decided to go on.

Putting the ptarmigan into a pocket, I started off due south. Ben walked slowly at my side. I kept a firm grip on the lead and felt very thankful that he had had the temerity to follow me; his company now was most welcome. Various thoughts struck me uncomfortably as I picked my way forward, one of which was that, should the mist continue so dense, it would be quite possible to pass the croft within a few yards and remain unaware of having done so. I held out my free arm and was just able to see the tips of my fingers; beyond them all was covered as though by a white blanket. I began to feel very cold and tired, but the tiredness was almost certainly due to fear allied with having to concentrate continuously in order to keep going in what I hoped was a southerly course. I had been feeling quite fresh in the corrie. I strove hard to keep calm and not panic, though if I relaxed the hold on myself a moment, fear welled up and vitiated mental and bodily energy.

Time as reckoned by men in minutes and hours began to

lose meaning and I found it increasingly difficult to calculate even approximately how long I had been walking since the mist descended, and how far I had come—half a mile, two miles? I had no idea. Telling myself that it was necessary to keep my circulation going, I started to run. Ben dragged back on the lead. There was a squelch as I stepped up to my ankles in bog. During the ensuing seconds, after I had hastily stepped out again, I lost every vestige of a sense of direction. North, south, east or west, I was quite ignorant in which direction I faced. What little common sense I had left told me to stay on the relatively stable piece of ground on to which I had stepped back, and sit there until the mist lifted, exposure now being the lesser danger. Yet I felt I could not bear to remain much longer in this spot surrounded by invisible quagmires.

On walks with Ben I would often call "Home!" to him when the time came to retrace my steps, so that he would know I was returning. Now I spoke this word to him and trusted he would have the initiative to take upon himself the task of leading us back to the croft. For what seemed ages he continued to sit without making a move.

"Home!" I repeated urgently.

At last he got up and with no sign of hurry began to walk forward; I followed, clinging to the lead as a drowning person might cling to a length of driftwood. We continued to walk forwards at a slow pace. As the damp grasses flicked round my ankles I expected at any moment to sink into a morass. We reached firmer ground, where the grass grew shorter and more wiry, and I began to breathe more easily. Ben meandered round rocks, sometimes turning right, sometimes left, in a most haphazard manner, until in desperation I was on the point of taking over leadership again. But I stopped myself from doing so; he had got us out of the bogland, now let him get us home,

I told myself. Though we seemed to be circling badly I came to lose all feelings of anxiety as I placed the responsibility of a safe homecoming on Ben's shoulders. Our walk through the mist began to have a dreamlike, unending quality. The rear portions of Ben's anatomy were visible to me, his forequarters and head faded into the mist. Presently a dim sense of recognition possessed me although I could still only see Ben's nether regions and a few feet of grass. Then my left hand touched stone—a wall—and turning my head I could just see a faint light shining from behind a window. Still leading, Ben walked through the open door of the croft. We were home, yet strangely I had no great feeling of relief. That was felt by Aunt Miriam who, since the mist had enveloped the countryside, had sat in the croft acutely anxious, knowing that it would be quite useless to go and look for me.

As I sat in the glow of the lamplight spooning up hot soup and clad in dressing-gown and slippers I suddenly remembered the ptarmigan. I had taken off my dress and hung it up in the cupboard, forgetful of the wee bird. He proved to be a hardy specimen and was still very much alive. Unwrapping him from the handkerchief I administered a few drops of warm milk and put him into a cage. Owing to the circumstances of my homecoming my crime in removing him from the nest was hardly commented upon by Aunt.

This young bird, which I named Jim, was successfully reared. Every three hours during the day he received a small quantity of heather shoots and chopped fresh berries. Ptarmigan are almost exclusively vegetarian. In the evenings he was let out of his cage and flew about the parlour. He developed into a fine bird with a bright red comb over his eyes. When he was about six weeks old he was released.

As I was of a somewhat superstitious nature in those days,

Ben's feat of homefinding in the mist began to appear to me in retrospect as an act imbued with an almost occult significance. It was the only time he had followed me against orders and it so happened that this was the only occasion I had got well and truly lost. Aunt Miriam too was much impressed with his prowess, but she rejected my suggestion that he had hurried after me in the role of a self-constituted guardian, having had a premonition that I would run into danger while out on the walk.

Whether Ben possessed psychic powers or not he certainly possessed great intelligence and a better knowledge of the hills than we did. Of the dogs I have owned since none has had such character as he nor been endowed with such tremendous energy. In view of our warm feelings towards him what occurred a short while later was for us a tragedy.

We made the most of the long summer evenings, seldom going to bed much before half-past eleven. Yet it was about this time, when we were preparing for bed, that Ben would start to get restless. If the doors and parlour windows were shut he would spring on to the window ledge and stare out, now and then giving a whine of impatience. Directly a window or door was opened he would be out and away. Sometimes he reappeared after we had finished breakfast, his coat darkened with sweat, and flopped down exhausted to sleep until midday. At other times he would return in the early hours before dawn had broken. That summer he seldom took himself off to the hills during the day, but always went at night.

"We'll keep him in," said Aunt one evening, and although the weather was very warm, doors and parlour windows were kept shut. Ben's restlessness increased when he saw us going to bed without having opened a window for him. We decided he must have discovered a bitch several miles distant and that it was to her he went each night.

Some while after I had been in bed I got up and went into the parlour to fetch a glass of water. Ben was lying on the window ledge pressed against the panes. On seeing me he sprang down, sped swiftly into my room and made a getaway from my window. The following morning he returned as exhausted as usual.

Then on a certain afternoon Mr. McNairn walked into the croft, his rifle slung over his shoulder. Ben and the otters gathered round him and as he pulled an ear and stroked a back he explained the reason for his visit. A dog was chasing and mauling his sheep. So far he had not spotted it but he had his suspicions as to who the culprit was—the Frasers' mongrel collie, a ne'er-do-well in his estimation. Heated words had been exchanged between him and Mrs. Fraser, she denying vehemently that her dog would so much as sniff at a sheep. He had left her with the warning that he was keeping his gun loaded and would shoot any dog he saw in the vicinity of his flocks. He asked us to let him know if we should happen to see a strange dog roaming the hills, and we promised to do so.

Two days later as we were working in the croft garden I saw Mr. McNairn walking up the hill, his rifle slung over his shoulder as before. With sudden intuition Aunt Miriam glanced at Ben who was lying asleep on the wall, and said, "He's the culprit." And as she spoke these words I knew she was right. It seems incredible to me now that neither of us till that moment harboured the slightest suspicion that it was Ben who was guilty of chasing sheep.

Mr. McNairn pointed a finger at him when he reached the croft, saying, "I found a sheep which had been run to its death yesterday and early this morning I saw him through my glasses skivvering along Pollie Hill way." Ben was taken into the parlour and given an enema.

The result, which contained traces of sheep's wool, proved his guilt. There can be no reprieve for a dog which chases sheep. He was led off straightaway by Mr. McNairn and shot, his body being left unburied among the hills.

Aunt Miriam had to make good the loss of one sheep. As with other dogs which become addicted to sheep chasing, Ben had clung to the animal's throat as it ran until the wretched creature had died through asphyxiation, exhaustion and terror. Goodness knows how many others he had terrified and mauled before being found out. Latterly he had become canny, only indulging in his crime under cover of dark.

His unhappy rending filled us with gloom, and, to lower our spirits further, the weather broke the day after he had been shot and for almost a week rain fell with hardly a break in a steady, grey downpour. The goats stamped morosely in the byre, vegetables floated in pools of water and much of the garden soil was washed away. Every time we left the croft we had to garb ourselves in mackintoshes and gumboots. Then the rain suddenly stopped and the sky shone a clear blue, flecked with white clouds. We ceased talking about the advantages of civilisation in wet weather—visits to cinemas and cafes, friends in to tea—and cut slices of bread and cake, washed a marooned lettuce which I found halfway down the hill, and prepared to spend a day in the open.

"Another hour in the croft and I would have had a nervous breakdown," said Aunt Miriam.

Life up here got you like that sometimes.

We walked until we came to a stretch of the Blackwater. The river flowed swiftly, the heavens reflected on its surface. We turned up a tributary where the waters were more sluggish. On the banks grew willow, birch, rowan and alder; reeds and sedge spread in thick clumps from the sides of the burn. As we were eating our lunch we heard the high whistling sound which otters make to call each other. We sat quiet, hoping to get a glimpse of an otter family. Presently a head appeared through the reeds and the otter gave another whistle and came straight towards us. It was Hansel. Another moment passed and then Gretel appeared. They helped us finish lunch and followed us home. They were in their third year and wandering far from the croft. We knew that one day they would leave us for good.

Most years the hay was cut in July, raked over once or twice, depending on the weather, and then forked into conical stacks around the pikes. A fortnight or so later the pikes would be lifted and the hay forked into the trap, the pony being led to the byre where it was unloaded. Haymaking was not particularly onerous work. But digging peat was gruelling.

Two large wicker panniers were fixed on either side of the pony. We walked over to the peat hags wearing gum boots and carrying spades. During my first years at the croft I was not capable of digging peat at all, and my job was to lift the damp clogs and the panniers. Male visitors were always very welcome for they were much better at this form of labour than we were. Women, I find, can walk or climb as well as or sometimes better than men, but their arms very seldom attain the strength of a man's. I do not think our male guests enjoyed peat digging any more than we did, but we were careful to reward them with good meals and set them to more congenial tasks in between. The bricks of peat were layed out to dry and then stacked at the side of the byre. Peat digging, drying and stacking went on throughout the summer, a seemingly endless task.

In September we made a special trip to the township to send off Christmas presents to friends and relations, and to collect the Christmas presents we had ordered for one another by mail as well as yuletide fare and decorations likewise ordered.

Written on each package we sent off was the instruction that it was not to be opened till the twenty-fifth of December. It was, of course, often possible to make trips to the township during late autumn and winter but we could never be sure exactly when. On getting back home we wrapped up our presents and put them away in the dresser with the boxes of dates, preserved fruits, chocolates, nuts and raisins.

Towards the middle of September the evenings began to get noticeably shorter and the winds had an edge to them. We checked over supplies, looked out the bird box, and made sure that there were no crannies in byre or croft. Soon enough the gales would come roaring down the corries and we would wake one morning to find the ground covered with snow.

croft life in winter

Several of the friends who stayed with us during summer grew so enthusiastic about the life we were leading that they were all for throwing up their jobs, spending their savings on crofts and holdings, and living the simple life themselves. Aunt Miriam always did her best to dissuade these enthusiasts, begging them, before they bought a place, first to spend a winter in a croft.

A young married couple who had enjoyed a fortnight with us promptly went and bought a croft in Wester Ross soon after leaving, in spite of Aunt's pleadings that they should not. They 'escaped' from it, they told us later the following spring, having been unable to endure the life more than five months.

"It was the terrifying loneliness", they explained. "We began to feel if we didn't get away soon it would swamp us."

They were fortunate in being able to resell their croft. Really there are very few adults these days who possess the mental and emotional self-sufficiency necessary for leading satisfactory existences in these remote parts.

When the daylight lasts for only five or six hours, when the Never Silent—as the Norsemen called the wind—howls down the corries and the snow is lying so deep that even the deer are unable to reach the croft in search of food, then one learns what it means to be cut off from the outside world, and either one grows to accept and appreciate spells of complete isolation, or else the isolation begins to sap one's confidence and to terrify.

From mid-September to April or May we were alone in the croft, and for weeks, sometimes months, we saw nobody except each other. Even the postman was rarely able to call in during winter for a chat. The croft was at a fairly high altitude and we had snow every year. Yet on a sunny day with the snow lying on the hills and round the croft we would take a walk to a lower altitude and picnic on the grass. Some days in winter could be extraordinarily mild and pleasant.

As the hours of darkness lengthened our days became relatively shorter. We seldom rose before nine and were in bed by nine-thirty. Reading in bed was strictly forbidden because of using up too much paraffin. The only occasion I have ever known Aunt Miriam to smack an animal was when she discovered Hansel chewing up a precious packet of candles. What remained of them was scrupulously swept into a pan, melted down and re-formed into rough oblongs. We never wasted a scrap of candle-grease or drop of paraffin. When there was a heavy deluge of rain during winter only a thin light was able to penetrate the leaden sky, and the day was spent in semi-darkness. We cooked and ate by lamplight, religiously turned out the flame when the meal was finished, and allowed ourselves a brief two hours of light again after supper before turning in to bed. The animals' propensity for sleep through a spell of bad weather was remarkable. Except for the briefest exits to answer the calls of nature they would lie comatose for hours on couch, carpet, or in box, and were very little trouble. We cut their food down when they took next to no exercise.

Keeping goats and a pony meant that however treacherous

the weather there was always the necessity to cross over to the byre twice a day in order to milk, feed and water them. Even this short journey of ten strides could be arduous. Several times, to my delight, I watched Aunt from a window going along the path on hands and knees because the force of the gale prevented her from standing upright. I too had to take my turn at milking when one of these fierce gales was blowing and make my way across in this ignominious position, but it was never so funny then. When a gale was blowing hard from the east it was often impossible to open the back door and we were compelled to use the front one only. A strong westerly gale meant using the back door only. In this kind of blustery weather we never opened a window; we got all the fresh air we wanted on the brief crossings to and from the byre. After a heavy fall of snow during the night it would take us a hard morning's work to free the doors and dig a path from the croft to the byre. Our preliminary exit on these occasions had to be through a window because the weight of snow jammed the doors tight. Sometimes when it had been snowing for several days on end and the snow level reached eight or nine feet—up to the roof of the croft—we would dig in shifts from morning till late at night, working by lamplight, in order to keep the path clear and the windows free from the pressure of snow. Surrounding our domain would be an impenetrable white wall. I would stand on a box in the high narrow pathway we had cleared and stare over the snow wall across the white countryside, enjoying the sensation of being completely marooned and cut off from the rest of the world.

One of the most difficult lessons we had to learn was to be content to do very little, during winter especially, for quite long periods. From the merest toddlers it has been so dinned into us that we should be continuously busy throughout the day—Satan finds work for idle hands, and so on—that when one first attempts to discard these teachings and sit contentedly doing absolutely nothing it is by no means easy. The mind is both guilty and bored. But all tendencies to try filling in the idle minute must be rigorously suppressed. It is fatal, living in these parts, if the mind and hands are continually seeking for something to occupy them. When the stockings have been darned, the animals fed, the hour not yet come to light the lamp and read, then surely one should be able to sit for a while without feeling restless or guilty. Yet modern conditioning and upbringing have made the art of relaxing and emptying the mind of petty concerns and worries a feat difficult of attainment by most. Nevertheless we eventually learnt to accomplish it to the dismay of energetic friends when they came to stay.

"Don't you get bored stiff when you are snowed in?" they would ask.

"Never," we would assure them truthfully.

"What do you do when you've finished the chores?"

"Nothing much."

At this looks of deep suspicion would cross their faces. "I feel sure too long at this life wouldn't be good for one. Don't you find you reach a stage of not wanting to do anything"

"Yes."

Most animals enjoy playing in the snow. If it was not too deep the otters would race out when the flakes had stopped falling and roll over and over in it, then chase each other like dogs. As they had been reared in a croft from infancy I had to show them how to make a snow chute and slide down it. I chose a steep hill and beat a length of snow hard with a spade, making the first descent myself on a tin tray. The otters were not long in getting the hang of tobogganing. Soon they were flying down the chute, forepaws tucked well in to their sides, back legs

69

used for giving a brisk send-off and then kept out straight. No sooner had they reached the bottom than they hurried up to the top for another go. Lora was much slower to take to it than they were but tobogganing does not come so naturally to seals as to otters. She barked furiously at seeing Hansel and Gretel descending in quick succession but was too nervous for a long while to attempt a descent herself. Presently she tried a short slither but rapidly manoeuvred herself over to the side with her flippers, not caring for the sensation at all. I took an otter down with me on the tray. The other followed by itself closely behind. Lora was left alone at the top, barking her annoyance. I called to her. With obvious trepidation she ventured once more on to the slide, moved her foreflippers and was off to a slow start. Her pace increased swiftly. Her run ended in a great uprush of snow and the length of the chute was extended by several yards. After that initial slide she had no more fear of going down. The following morning, instead of making for the lochan as usual, she waddled straight up to the chute. She was only able to make comparatively few runs for it took her many minutes to reach the top again.

Not all the slides went smoothly. The otters were always pushing each other around at the top of the chute and taking playful snaps at one another. Once the heftier Hansel shoved Gretel off sideways and her descent was a series of rapid somersaults. On reaching the bottom she lay quite still for several seconds and when she eventually got up she staggered around in circles, quite overcome by dizziness. Another time Hansel started off just in front of Lora. Owing to her greater weight she soon overtook him and he was pushed forward at an increasing speed by her body. When the end of the chute was reached there was a piercing, blood curdling bark from Hansel as she swept right over him. Aunt and I, who happened to be watching from the top, both automatically put a hand across our eyes. I fully expected to see a flattened, defunct Hansel when I looked again. But his body possessed the qualities of India rubber and when I next glanced in his direction he was giving himself a shake and then running up the hill for yet another slide.

Even when the ice on the lochan was several inches thick we never ventured out on it ourselves. But the first job Lora and the otters set themselves to do on these wintry mornings was to free their plungeholes of the ice which had formed over them during the night. The otters would dab at the ice with their forepaws and press down with their bodies, and Lora would press down with her nose and foreparts. Both seals and otters have a wonderfully acute sense of direction. One year there was a plungehole—too small for Lora to enter—underneath the rock from which they dived. It was fascinating to watch the otters dive off with hardly a moment's hesitation and go straight through the hole. Its circumference did not appear to be much larger than their bodies. After a swim under the ice-covered water they would reappear again up the hole, having found it, apparently, without any difficulty. Once, watching through fieldglasses, I saw Lora disappear through a plungehole towards the centre of the lochan and her head reappear through it six minutes later. An otter's sense of direction on land is as unerring as it is in water and it will return to old holts and use the same trails, though it may not have travelled them for months and years. It is often supposed that birds such as grouse and ptarmigan, which dwell in high moorland areas, are so well adapted to their environment that they suffer no casualties during a spell of severe weather. But, well adapted though they are both by behaviour and plumage, the weather takes its toll. We used to go out with a basket during severe spells of weather and collect what bird casualties we could find. Although such birds as thrushes and blackbirds would be in the majority we not infrequently picked up grouse and ptarmigan, suffering from exposure or starvation or a combination of both.

Should the weather permit, sometimes in mid-December we used to walk down to a spinney. In it were several holly bushes and trees whose trunks were covered with ivy. We returned home carrying strands of ivy and bunches of holly with which to decorate the croft at Christmas.

In the past the holly was regarded as a 'lucky' tree, while the ivy was believed to be a plant liable to bring misfortune. These three verses from an old carol dating from the fifteenth century express the feelings our ancestors had for the holly and the ivy.

> *Holly and his merry men they dance and they sing,*
> *Ivy and her maidens they weep and they wring,*
> *Ivy hath a kybe; she suffers from the cold,*
> *So must they all that with Ivy hold.*

> *Holly hath berries as red as any rose,*
> *The forester and the hunter keep them from the does.*
> *Ivy hath berries as black as any sloe,*
> *There comes the wolf and eats them as she goes.*

> *Holly hath birds, a full fair flock,*
> *The Nightingale, the Poppingy, the gentle Laverock.*
> *Good Ivy! What birds has thou?*
> *None but the Howlet that cries 'How! how!'*

(A kybe is a chilblain. The Poppingy and Laverock are the woodpecker and lark.)

Our third winter at the croft was the worst we ever experienced, It had started off well. Throughout September and the first two weeks in October we were still going for long walks in the higher hills and picnicking at lower altitudes. Then one day towards the end of October the sky had that dark steely look which betokens a cold spell. No rain fell and there was little breeze but it continued to get colder and colder. The goats and pony, which up till then had been staked out on the turf, were led into the byre. We filled up bins and scuffles with peat and coal and stacked more peat by the front and back doors. Buckets were filled with water from the stream, two for the croft and two for the byre. It got so cold during the night that we both had to get up to close our windows and put more blankets on the beds. Small gritty nodules of snow and ice rattled against the panes. For three days a blizzard raged. All that could be seen from the windows were the dark shapes of the hills and the byre and a white ground haze. The cold was so bitter that on returning from the short journey to the byre our fingers were numb and rigid. To fetch more water from the stream was an agonising task, for apart from the cold the gale lashed stinging grains of icy snow against face and hands. One evening I left half a bucket of milk over in the byre and the following morning it was frozen solid. It became so gloomy sitting in the croft listening to the high-pitched whine of the gale and the incessant swish of the frozen nodules against the panes that we kept the lamp burning all day.

On the fourth day the gale abated and large flakes of snow began to whirl down. The cold was still intense but against all our inclinations we forced ourselves to start digging a path round the croft and over to the byre. Twenty minutes of digging was all that we could stand and then we came in and revived ourselves with cups of tea before recommencing shovelling snow again.

Snow reached the level of the eaves but we managed to keep pace with it. Three feet from the croft was an encircling wall, the top surface extending outwards across the countryside, the inner sloping away slightly from the croft and beaten hard with the flat of the spade to prevent toppling and crumbling. The path between croft and wall which ran out to the byre was the only stretch of ground on which we could walk. When the drifts were so high and it was impossible to fetch water from the stream we scooped snow up in buckets from the top of the wall and melted it down on the range.

Once or twice a day we cautiously raised the lid of the bird-box, which was placed on the lee of the croft in order to make sure that none of the birds which had sought sanctuary in it was ailing. It was difficult to see them among the thick straw and extract the invalids without frightening the rest. The small china bin was refilled with grain and bits of fat and the lid closed again. On the lee of croft and byre birds would crouch in the snow under the shelter of the eaves, the gap between snow and eaves being only a few inches. Each morning we found casualties, dead birds and others which were very weakly. Of those we were able to reach we put the ones suffering from exposure into a lidded basket. Some lying stiff and cold appeared to be dead but it was not easy to tell at a glance whether a spark of life might not still be flickering in them. After one morning's collection, just as she was re-entering the croft, Aunt Miriam happened to notice a wren almost covered with fresh fallen snow. When she picked it up it seemed to be dead, then she thought she detected a faint sign of life so put it in the basket with the rest. Besides the wren, there were ten other birds in the basket; a stonechat, twite, three blackbirds, two thrushes, a snow bunting, starling, and chaffinch.

First aid was administered on a table in Aunt's bedroom.

The birds were placed round an oil-lamp and the gentle heat gradually restored their circulation. The inert bodies would become warmer to the touch, a wing would move slightly, faint cheeps grow louder and break into twitters. Those which revived were put into cages, the smaller birds being kept separate from the larger. A few drops of warm milk were forcibly administered. Bins of bread-and-milk and scraps of fat were put in each cage, then green felt was laid over the wire-meshed front to keep out light and induce the invalids to sleep. Of that particular batch the starling died and it appeared unlikely that the wren would recover. It lay with its little eyes half open, not moving at all. The birds that were seriously ill were laid, after a period of thawing by the lamp, in boxes of appropriate size on top of dolls' hot-water bottles. I had brought a collection of these bottles of various sizes with me to the croft and they proved most useful for keeping warm seriously ailing small mammals and birds.

One of these bottles was filled with hot water, a piece of flannel wrapped round it, the wren laid on top and bottle and wren inserted into an old powder box. The worst of these dolls' bottles was that they cooled off rapidly and had to be constantly refilled. Although it was in such a feeble state, Aunt squeezed several drops of milk down the wren's throat via a pen-dipper, the milk having been mixed with a minute quantity of brandy.

I happened to go into the parlour while this operation was taking place to fetch another piece of flannel for laying over the wren. Whilst in there I distinctly heard two taps on the pane. So did the otters for they woke at once from their doze and stared fixedly at the window. The taps were repeated and I thought I saw something white move outside. The chances of its being a ghost or banshee did not strike me as being beyond the bounds of possibility. Far from it. My legs suddenly felt very weak, yet I managed to make a speedy return to Aunt's room and inform her that something white was tapping on the parlour window. Without any ado, she went and opened it. Flakes of snow blew into the parlour and with them fluttered a white ptarmigan. (The plumage of these birds changes to white during winter, with a few bars of black on tail and wings.) The bird flew to the dresser and after walking along the top rail flew down and lighted on Aunt's shoulder. He appeared to be quite at his ease.

"Could it be Jim?" said Aunt.

Sure enough, it was. When I brought out a tin from the dresser containing sultanas he flew over to me at once. He used to be given a sultana as a treat occasionally in the past. Directly the lid was removed he poked his neck into the tin and helped himself.

Jim stayed with us three days until the worst of the weather was over. Then we opened a window and he flew out. We never saw him again.

The wren hovered between life and death for two days. Every four hours it received drops of warmed milk. Then on the third day it perked up in the space of a few minutes and made a quick recovery. It sat in its box and fluffed out its feathers, uttering sharp cries of "tick, tick!" Presently it hopped on to the edge of the box and started to clean its breast feathers. Although wrens are insect-eating birds it ate the bread-and-milk it was offered. Later it received scraps of fat and meat. It never showed the slightest fear of either of us and was allowed the freedom of the bedroom when no animal was about.

It is always a pleasure when the things pertaining to invalidism can be put away and one can watch and listen to former sufferers pecking up morsels of food from one's hand and singing and chirping gaily. Hearing birds indoors one realises the strength and carrying power of their voices. When the wren uttered its sharp "tick, tick" in Aunt's bedroom it could be heard clearly in the parlour with both doors closed. We were treated to brilliant displays of singing by thrushes and blackbirds, but these songsters are best enjoyed in the open for their voices are too powerful indoors. Directly there was a break in the weather those birds which had recovered sufficiently were let out. Many we never saw again but others revisited the croft, some almost daily.

Our circle of bird friends grew like a chain letter, a bird which we had cared for during a blizzard returning later, for example, with one or two acquaintances of its species. We often got back to the croft after a walk to find, if a door or window had been left open, several of our late guests disporting themselves on picture frames and furniture while nervous newcomers flew agitatedly round the room, uttering cries of alarm at our entry. A healthy bird is as inquisitive and full of vitality as a healthy mammal and it can be very destructive. We returned one day to discover artificial flowers in a bowl pecked to pieces, and a china ornament knocked off the mantelpiece and broken. A starling was on the writing desk and, having chattered a brief greeting to us, it continued with the task of extracting envelopes from a packet and dropping them over the side of the desk. It had upset the inkwell—probably by hopping up on to it—and from the desk descended a stream of ink upon the carpet. As it had walked over the white tablecloth, spread for tea, its ink-stained claws had made a delicate winding pattern which several washings failed to remove.

The various disadvantages connected with birds entering the croft were more than compensated for by the charm of their company.

Deer often came down to the croft in severe weather in search of food, their lean flanks showing the effects of poor grazing. There was nothing we could do for them. The cold seemed to make them tamer; they would stand about watching us, their breath streaming white from their nostrils, and allow us to approach to within quite a short distance before moving slowly off. One day when I was sitting in the parlour I was frightened on hearing a loud snort followed by an antlered head appearing through the window. The stag regarded me calmly for a while then withdrew. Red deer, except in the pairing season, roam in herds of one sex, the calves running with the hinds until the males are old enough to join the stags.

On Christmas Eve we decorated the croft with greenery, clipped candles to a small artificial fir and hung coloured glass balls and lengths of tinsel on the branches. The tree was placed on top of the piano whose straight, varnished sides were beyond Sara's climbing powers. On our first Christmas at the croft we had unthinkingly placed a real fir, appropriately decorated, on a cane table. Hearing an ominous splintering of glass, we rushed into the parlour to find a silver ball lying broken on the floor and the tree rocking back and forth precariously as the two squirrels clung to its branches and busily gnawed off twigs and chewed up candles. Cuthbert had managed to get himself entwined with tinsel and it was several minutes before we were able to free him. This tree always fascinated Sara and every year she made strenuous efforts to reach it. As she sat on the arm of a chair and contemplated its decorated branches it was almost possible to read her mind at work on various methods of approach. She stood on her hind legs at various positions round the piano, her forepaws pressed against the varnished sides. At each failure to ascend her chittering grew louder and more angry. Then one Christmas she succeeded in reaching her objective. The fir was on the top of the piano as usual. She had tried different ways of reaching it, all of which had ended in failure. Then, via the picture rail, she managed to climb down the wire supporting a picture and gain a foothold on the frame. Struggling valiantly along a piece of holly she eventually managed to reach another bit protruding from a picture immediately above the piano. There was a plop as she landed on the piano top, and then, before either of us were able to reach her, she ascended the tree on which the candles were lit and blazing merrily. Fortunately she did not singe herself and, even more fortunately, did not knock the tree over. After this effort of hers we decided that henceforth there must be no lighted candles on the fir.

With an open range and oil-lamps and no fire brigade handy we had to be very careful about placing a guard in front of the range and keeping lamps and exposed flames out of reach of the animals.

Our Christmas lunch consisted most years of mushroom soup concocted from mushrooms we had picked and dried during autumn; tinned turkey, oats and bottled carrots; Christmas pudding and hard sauce, followed by preserves, nuts and chocolates. And for drink, home-made sloe wine.

We put out an extra quantity of food for the birds on Christmas morning, looking on them as our guests, as no human friends were able to visit us. Each animal was given a treat in the way of food. A tin of sardines was opened for Lora and the otters. Rodney and Sara had nuts and raisins. We unwrapped presents received from friends months before as well as those sent especially for an animal. Rodney received his felt balls and one year a package addressed to Lora was found to contain a drum and beater, sent by a young cousin of mine.

"Oh, horror!" said Aunt Miriam, opening it. "Shall we give it to her?"

Much to our relief, Lora effectively rendered this gift useless by sitting on the vellum, which promptly tore.

"Has she learnt to play the drum yet?" came an inquiry by post the following spring.

"I'm sorry to have to tell you…" I wrote back.

Another letter in reply to mine was received in due course. "Never mind," wrote the kindly donor, "I'm saving up to buy her another."

neighbours and visitors

On going to the stream one summer morning, bucket in hand, I saw to my surprise at the rear of a boulder a white bell tent. A figure presently emerged clad in shorts, checked shirt and a turban; he politely took the bucket from me and filled it at the stream. As we walked back to the croft I learnt that he and his brother—still asleep in the tent—were the sons of an Indian friend of my father's and were studying in England. They had successfully found their way to us with the aid of map and compass and a sheaf of instructions from Aunt Emily. A letter announcing their arrival reached us two weeks later, having in the meantime travelled around Sunderland, to which county they had addressed it.

Ram and Narshidas had thoughtfully stowed away packets of photographs of their homeland in their mountainous ruck-sacks. My parents had spent the greater part of their lives in India and I had been born out there in the province of Orissa, so it gave me great delight to look at the snaps which included several of the beautiful Nilgiri Hill district where we had lived for several years. The jungle-clad slopes were in direct contrast to the bare hills of Sutherland but equally compelling in their way.

Indians seldom become addicted to European food. The brothers had brought with them packets of rice and tins of curry powder, and we supplied them with milk and vegetables. As Aunt Miriam and I ate our sober hotpot, Ram and Narshidas would be eating an exotic-looking curry. They asked us one day if we would like to try one and to this suggestion we readily assented.

From a handful of carrots, several onions, a few herbs and red currants—the only fruit we grew—they made a magnificent curry which took them the best part of an evening to prepare. At the end of it we were left gasping for breath, but we were assured by the cooks that it was not nearly so fiery as most Indian curries.

They told us that they had found Lora in their tent when they returned to it after breakfast one morning, and it had taken them a long time to entice her out. Aunt Miriam asked if any damage had been done.

"She went in only to observe," Narshidas replied, from which we gathered that no belongings had been gnawed or squashed.

Lora took a great fancy to Ram. She would sit by the tent in the early mornings waiting for him to emerge, whereupon she would drop a pebble or bit of stick at his feet as an offering. Only a few visitors were treated to this sign of her affections.

This habit of picking up some object and dropping it at the favoured one's feet is also common to dogs. On a master's return to the house a dog will often snatch up a handy object then drop it in front of the master as a means of showing its pleasure. I have a friend who once owned a cocker spaniel. The dog, which slept in her room, would jump out of the window each morning and take himself for a run. He would pick up a pebble from the gravel path, spring back through the window and on to his mistress's bed, where he would deposit the pebble on the eiderdown. If the gift was not promptly acknowledged by the sleepy mistress, the dog would drop the pebble on her head. He was, she assured me, more effective than an alarm clock.

Mr. McNairn called while our Indian guests were with us and we were astonished to hear him telling them that as a youth he had sailed to Ceylon and India in a trading vessel. He, for his part, was equally astonished to hear that my earliest years had been spent in India. In spite of being neighbours, we had been quite unaware until then of these facts about each other. Mr. McNairn had an appearance which belied him. With his white beard, brown, strangely unlined face, his slow, gentle way of speaking and his stately walk and gestures he reminded me of a venerable wise man and I would never have suspected him of having strayed so far from his homeland. But his whole youth, we learnt later, had been spent on the seas and travelling in the East. It was not until he was nearing forty that he had returned to Scotland and taken up shepherding.

When we first knew him he was in his mid sixties. As he regarded one with blue, far-seeing eyes one got the feeling that he might have the gift of second sight. Fortunately I did not ask him whether he possessed it and it was not long before I discovered that Mr. McNairn, unlike many a highlander, could not abide any 'aery faery talk' as he called it.

When I visited him in his two-roomed croft the conversation centred on such topics as animals and their doings, ceilidhs he had been to in his youth, and bits of news in a local paper sent by a relation in Ullapool. Spells, fairies, and the second sight were topics which held no attraction for him. These visits I paid him were always chancy affairs. It took me over an hour to reach his croft and then there was the possibility that he would be out. But should I find him in I could be sure of a lengthy chat and a cup of tea. There would be a kettle on the sworlie and the black cat, Tim, grooming itself by the hearth. There was nothing in the tiny parlour to give a clue to Mr. McNairn's travels in the past, nor were there any photographs of friends or relations.

"I've never been one for keepsakes or snaps," he once remarked. "My auld grannie lost a woollen shawl when I was a boy which had been knitted by her mother and a' of the family were kept busy a whole day looking for it. Wha' a stramash over a shawl! That learnt me not to put much store by any object. Twa days later it was found over in the byre where the cat had dragged it to make a warm nest for its kittens. The shawl looked a wee bit wearie by then. 'I knew some body had snitched it,' said Grannie. 'Well she can keep it now but skivvering off wie it like that I'll no bury her decent when she dees but skin her and make a fur collar of her coat.' Aye, and she did too."

Of his possessions there were two, I felt, he put some store by, however; one was a dirk which he said his family had had since the Rising in 1745. The only time I ever saw him look guilty was when I happened to enter his croft and found him using the dirk to stir a bowl of sheeps' liniment. The other possession I think he secretly treasured was his pipes, of which he was no mean player. Much as he enjoyed 'fashioning music', though, his greatest pleasure was reading. Against one side of his parlour was a bookshelf stacked with eclectic rows of volumes on theology, biology, sheep-rearing and history, as well as novels and volumes of poetry. His favourite poet was Rob Donn whose verse he would recite on request.

Donn, who is buried in Balnakeill churchyard, is the most celebrated poet of the Reay country. He was an anomalous character, for, in spite of not being able to read or write, he composed profusely. A fervent Jacobite, he wrote several poems in praise of Prince Charlie, but the majority are songs of the shieling, wool-waulking and other simple country activities. Owing to his Celtic blood, many of his poems have a strain of sadness running through them.

Between Mr. McNairn's croft and the Frasers' was a series of low hills, and winding through the shallow valleys was a stretch of grass differing from the surrounding grasslands in that it was of a deeper green and lusher. It made me wonder whether it had once been used a good deal as a track, decades back when the area had been more densely populated. Dotted singly along its length were rowan trees. These trees used to be planted near a croft as they were thought to give powerful protection against the forces of evil. But these trees apart, I could find no evidence of vanished crofts.

It was the short and swippert (quick and lithe) Mr. Fraser, whose words poured from him in rapid sentences which stopped suddenly like a stream plunged underground, who was the seer and spellbinder.

"Mr. Fraser!" I exclaimed in surprise when someone informed me that he was a wise man of renown, and that even in these scientific days people came long distances to seek his advice or ask him to put a spell on a sick animal for its recovery. I had always imagined a wise man with a fluffy white beard and blue, far-seeing eyes like Mr. McNairn's. Mr. Fraser was clean-shaven and his brown eyes were as quick moving as a town-dweller's. His manner did not exude a patriarchal calm but was inclined to be erratic. He had a sharp temper which soon cooled. If a conversation amused him he would laugh uproariously. If, on the other hand, it bored him he did not trouble to hide the fact. As for traditional highland hospitality— well, that depended where Mr. Fraser was concerned.

None could be more liberal with food and drink than he if he had taken a fancy to a person or was in the right mood, but otherwise the unexpected guest was liable to depart with his thirst unquenched.

"I'll no soak a leaf o' my tea for ye," he once shouted to a man who had travelled fifteen miles to see him, and to whom he had taken an unaccountable dislike.

On one of the first visits I paid him I found on my arrival that his wife was away in the hills and he busy with a sick cow in the byre.

"Ye'll hae to brew your own tea if ye want any," he informed me bluntly, adding—"and bring me out a cup when it's brewed."

While he was pouring a concoction down the cow's throat, I kept calling out questions about where the cups and the tea caddie were kept, while he shouted back the answers. At last the tea was made.

"Well, neither o' us will get tannin poisoning when we've drunk tha' brew," he commented, glancing at the anaemic looking liquid.

Nowadays, when a belief in the occult is often openly derided, it is difficult to get those who still believe in immaterial worlds and beings to talk about such subjects, and even when they do they are careful to pretend that they themselves take such 'unco' things only with a large pinch of salt. Fear of being scoffed at by a younger and more sceptical generation accounts for this attitude. Also, those whose eyes can penetrate the unseen do so only to a relatively small extent and their belief in the occult is therefore lightly held.

What interested me about those who visited Mr. Fraser—young and old, staunch disbelievers in Tir-nan-Og land of the fairies—was that the process was reversed, and they were careful not to incur scorn by exposing their scepticism in his presence. For Mr. Fraser accepted fairies and the efficacy of spells in the same way as others accept the power of electricity. He did not believe so much as know, and therein lay his strength. It had the effect of making even the most hardened materialist wonder whether perhaps there might not be something in it...

Mr. Fraser's father had come from Wester Ross and his mother was also from the west, hailing from Tiree in the Outer Hebrides. When he was seven the family moved to Sutherland and he had never once left its borders since. Both his parents held reputations as healers and seers. As is the custom in northern Scotland and the Hebrides, occult information is passed down from father to daughter and mother to son. So it was with him; he was instructed by his mother, and his sister by her father. Apart from the practice of healing and spellbinding, both he and his sister learnt from their parents by word of mouth 376 stories, some of which, he informed me, took over an hour in the telling. For, besides being a wise man, Mr. Fraser was one of the last traditional storytellers. Now that he is dead most of those old tales have died with him—tales that were passed down through the generations, from parent to child. I have often regretted since that I did not ask him to recount more of them.

Though so expert in the use of spells, Mr. Fraser was no faddist and he kept a good stock of medicines—both for human and animal use—in a wooden box in the byre.

"There's nothing like helping medicine along wie a spell or a spell wie a teaspoon o' medicine," was his advice.

"Him away over there—daft!" he was fond of exclaiming, indicating the direction of Mr. McNairn' s croft. Mr. McNairn was the only person I came across who told Mr. Fraser to his face that he considered spells to be outmoded. They made excellent neighbours. A stramash now and then only served to add to their respect for one another, and their widely differing views on life kept them sparring happily for years.

Mrs. Fraser was as unconventional and gifted as her husband. Her skill at knitting was formidable. She could walk beside one keeping up an animated conversation, and at the same time knitting a complicated pattern or turning the heel of a sock. In the evenings, if she was working on a garment that was not too tricky, she would close her eyes for half an hour or so and continue to ply the needles. Her more complicated efforts, done in a variety of colours and stitches, used to have me gaping in respectful admiration. I am myself, perhaps, the world's most inexpert knitter. The two jumpers I have made in the course of a lifetime both took me over a year to finish. My third jumper the moths finished before I did. Foolishly, I once challenged Mrs. Fraser to a knitting race which was to last ten minutes. When the time was up she had completed ten rows and I was still in the middle of my first.

Mrs. Fraser's chief talent, however, was as a singer of mouth music.

As the men and women tended the cattle or worked about the croft they used to sing, unaccompanied by any instrument, songs relating to crofting life—urging an obstinate cow over a stream, weaving, fishing, rocking the bairn to sleep. Many of these songs are of great beauty, but to my mind half their charm is lost when they are heard away from their natural setting. I still remember with a shudder a grim afternoon spent listening to mouth music in a hall in Glasgow. The performance was in aid of a charity—of course. But why people should be subjected to several hours' torture, and then have money extracted from them is beyond me. At the back of the hall was a display of ghastly gifties of the sort which are seen in the shops during summer to tempt luckless tourists—china Scottish terriers wearing tartan caps, miniature sgian dubhs, eagles' claws topped by imitation topaz—and these the audience were inveigled into buying. Then the concert started. A regal-looking woman in a black evening dress complete with tartan sash treated us to three unaccompanied songs. Her place was then taken by a male singer, likewise in full evening attire, who—also unaccompanied—gave a hearty rendering of 'Calling Cackie through the Watter' followed by a lament for a long-deceased Hebridean chief. A tea break came next, during which the last of the gifties were sold off at bargain prices to the fury of those who had bought some of these horrors earlier on. We returned to our hard wooden seats to listen to unaccompanied duets by the two performers. The afternoon ended with an encore, which as far as I can remember was entitled 'Wearily, drearily'. I felt the cap should have been passed round on behalf of the audience for enduring the concert with such heroic patience.

When Mrs. Fraser sang, her voice among the hills was as beautiful and appropriate as the cry of a bird. Although untrained professionally, her voice was true and of a remarkable clarity. How many songs did she know? "Oh, around sixty."

Soon the only way we shall be able to hear these songs will be in those dismal halls for which they are so unsuited, sung by persons who have little knowledge of croft life. For the younger generation of crofting folk seldom bother to learn the old songs and stories, though it is only from their lips that they have any true meaning and beauty.

Mrs. Fraser had been reared, she told me, on brose. This used to be the traditional fare of crofters. It consisted of oatmeal flavoured with salt, soaked in milk and boiling water. On this inadequate diet, served three times a day with only occasional additions of meat and vegetables, she had attained healthy womanhood. Apart from a few minor ailments, her health was excellent throughout her life and she possessed abundant energy. Perhaps there is something to be said for brose, though it seems likely in her case that fresh air and a slower tempo of living than most enjoy played a bigger part in creating her sound constitution than an oatmeal diet.

One summer Aunt Miriam received a letter from a friend asking if we would put up a Canadian couple for a week. They were both of Scottish extraction and were anxious to spend a time in a remote part of their ancestral homeland. We awaited their arrival with a certain amount of trepidation, wondering whether two sophisticated visitors from Toronto would fit into croft life.

When the Dacys arrived, having endured on the latter part of their journey seven miles of jolting in a wagon, their enthusiasm was not dampened at all. They assured us that they could quite easily squeeze into the minute spare bedroom and were looking forward to helping us about the croft.

After supper we sat outside chatting. Soft air blew through the grasses and a line of stags moved slowly over the crest of a distant hill. All was peace and beauty. Our animals had taken themselves out of sight and were apparently occupied with their own doings. Saying that the spell of the highlands had already gripped them, our guests went off to bed.

Sometimes on summer evenings the approach of night was barely perceptible. The moon rose to replace the sun and with its coming a different spirit—mysterious and utterly calm—penetrated the hills, but the colouring of the night sky differed little from that of evening. So it was, on that particular night.

Aunt Miriam and I strolled about long after our guests had gone to bed. It must have been past twelve when we eventually decided to retire ourselves. I had changed into a nightdress and was dawdling around the room. Suddenly the silence was pierced by a woman's scream so fearful that for several seconds I was literally rooted to the spot. More high-pitched screams followed from the direction of the Dacys' bedroom and were interspersed with gruff, panic-stricken shouts. When my mind, stunned into momentary blankness, began to function again, the first thought which arose in it was that the Dacys must have knocked over their paraffin lamp and that the croft was now ablaze. Then came a scream so eerie and fraught with terror that I concluded I had been wrong in my surmise. Some un-imaginable horror must have crawled over the Dacys' window and into their room. As far as the Dacys were concerned, this latter conjecture of mine proved correct. Ever of a cautious nature, I waited until I heard the sounds of Aunt's door being flung open and her bare feet running across the parlour before I followed in her wake.

A perplexing sight met our eyes. Mrs. Dacy, wearing a chiffon nightdress, was crouched in the square window space, effectively blocking out the moonlight. A torch shone on the carpet where it had apparently been dropped. Mr. Dacy, clad in pyjamas, was standing on top of the chest of drawers. Both were quite speechless from terror when we entered at the double. Aunt picked up the torch and flashed it about the room. The only object it revealed which could conceivably have caused the panic was Rodney, sitting on the bed lethargically cleaning his whiskers.

"Is that what's——?"

Mr. Dacy indicated by a brief gesture that it was. Aunt Miriam turned her attention to Mrs. Dacy who was still crouched precariously in the window space.

"But, Mrs. Dacy—it's only a rat!"

This remark of Aunt's effectively restored Mrs. Dacy's speech. "Did you say only a rat, Miss Farre?"

We were apt to forget that rats on the loose do not appeal to everyone.

I picked up Rodney who had curled up on the bed, and shut him in my room. When I returned the Dacys had descended from their eyries and Mrs. Dacy was telling Aunt in a shaking voice, which nevertheless had a note of rightful fury, how, having been sound asleep, she had woken with a start to feel something warm and furred brush past her face. Her husband, sleeping beside her, woke too, and then... She appeared over-come once more as she recollected what had occurred.

"Don't try and say any more, dear. Sit down."

"You tell them, Elwin," said Mrs. Dacy, sinking onto the bed.

"We both felt small paws and a tail move over our heads. I could make out some sort of an animal and when I switched on my torch there was this rat sitting on the sheet turn-over just above us. We naturally took a dive beneath the bedclothes, but then..." He also sat down beside his wife. "There must have been a gap somewhere because it came right in after us."

"Elwin, I shall have to ask you to stop."

"Yes, dear. I once met up with bugs in a log cabin but I've never been any place where there's been rats."

"Rodney's a tame rat," I ejaculated, not liking to hear him coupled with bed bugs.

"Tame or not tame, I don't care for rats running about the house or under the covers," said Mr. Dacy firmly.

Aunt apologised profusely. "It shan't happen again, I promise you."

"Well, I think, Miss Farre, that we will leave tomorrow," said Mrs. Dacy with finality. "I'm sure you understand."

As Mr. Dacy tenderly laid a silk dressing-gown over his wife's shoulders I was made aware that we were clad only in night-dresses and pyjamas. In our haste none of us had even pulled on a pair of slippers.

"Tea," murmured Aunt.

"You see," she explained, as, slippered and dressing gowned, we sat drinking that highland palliative for all ills, "it's four miles to Mr. McNairn. If he's in he generally volunteers to walk the two miles to the Frasers and Mr. Fraser then has an hour's walk to the man who owns the wagon to find out from him when he can come over with it to our croft. Things can't be arranged quickly up here, I'm afraid."

"Well, Elwin's a good walker. He'll be able to reach the man's croft by midday and get him to come hack with the wagon—won't you, Elwin?"

I thought I detected a flicker of doubt in her husband's eyes but he replied promptly enough that he would set out at the crack of dawn.

The following morning, accompanied by me, he started off. Three miles of tramping over a seemingly endless switchback of hills had him confessing that he was very sorry indeed in having to leave after so short a stay, and did I think Mr. McNairn would walk to the next croft as his own leg muscles were a little out of training? We sat down on a boulder and took a rest. The weather broke over our heads, and as neither of us had a mackintosh we were drenched in less than a minute.

"Wouldn't there be a danger of stepping into a bog with the rain coming down like this? I can't see more than a yard ahead."

"Yes," I replied without hesitation.

"You couldn't promise to keep that rat shut up if we stayed on?"

I assured him I could. We both turned and started to squelch back.

Rodney spent a somewhat confined week, but towards the end of it both the Dacys were able to insert crumbs through the wire mesh of his cage without flinching, and, moreover, were talking earnestly of returning to Britain in two years and renting a croft for a summer. It was with regret that we bade each other farewell.

I only twice met tinkers whilst living at the croft. Sutherland is not a county where they travel in any number. This family of seven, whose various relationships we were never able to sort out, camped by the side of the lochan. Every day men, women and children would come up to the croft to scrounge milk, food, and clothing. We grew weary of the incessant whine for goods, without any offer of payment by cash or labour. They had erected three bothies, made from bent saplings and lengths of sacking, one of which was pitched away from the other two. Squalor seemed to spring up around these people. A quick glance inside a bothie revealed squatting, unwashed figures surrounded by a jumble of tin cans, remnants of food and filthy coverings. Happening to look in the bothie pitched away from the other two, Aunt Miriam saw a woman lying in it clasping a newly-born child. It had been born, the woman said, the day before. She was separated from the rest because she must not use any of their pans or 'bed' coverings. Amongst her people women are considered unclean, she continued, during the menstrual period and after the birth of a child, until the discharge has cleared up. This belief is common among the more primitive peoples throughout the world, women being rigorously secluded from the rest of the family or tribe and the discomforts of their lives increased at the very time when they should have most care and attention. Three days later the father of the newborn child informed Aunt Miriam casually that they were moving on the next day in the direction of Lairg, the woman having 'picked up' sufficiently to make the journey possible. He was treated to a thrashing from Aunt's tongue with no effect whatsoever.

What sort of a man was he to let his wife give birth to a child with the minimum of attention, isolated in a bothie? It was the custom of his people, was the reply.

"Then it's high time the custom ended." He shrugged his shoulders. Did he realise that the woman was still weakly and unfit for walking any long distance?

"Oh, she could manage," was the laconic answer; "she has done it before."

It was with no regret that we saw them leave, though we were considerably troubled in our minds about the mother and infant. As I watched her dragging behind the rest, I would not have objected if some dictator had made a law that tinkers should be compelled to give up their way of life, move into council houses, and take regular work—and baths. My feelings towards tinkers then were anything but genial and their lives, so filled with dirt, poverty and squalor, seemed to me about the most unromantic it were possible to live. Years later I spent many months wandering with tinkers and gypsies, and my feelings towards them became more moderate. Individuals vary among them, of course, as much as they do among any other group of people. But my feelings are still the same towards that aspect of tinker life—now fortunately rapidly dying out—for it shows them to be ridden with the worst kind of superstition, and bears so adversely against the womenfolk.

folklore and legend

Sometimes I used to walk to an ancient forgotten well whose whereabouts had been revealed to me by Mr. Fraser. It was almost hidden among ferns and birch scrub and the stonework was covered with thick moss. Its waters had once been believed to have the power of curing ailments and granting wishes. It had also a less pleasant association, for in the past lunatics used to be dragged to it by ropes and forcibly ducked, in the hope that this would restore them to sanity. When I leaned over and dropped a coin into the dark waters and silently made a wish Mr. Fraser laughed heartily. He was no believer in wishing wells.

The occult is a tricky subject, and I am constantly surprised to find that some people will easily accept certain psychic phenomena whilst vehemently rejecting others. For myself, I am a firm believer in ghosts and banshees, and I can see no good reason—such is the power of thought—why spells and suchlike should not be very effective in bringing about the results for which they are cast. When more materialistic friends ask me how I can believe in such inanities as banshees my reaction is to say quietly but firmly that I consider it possible for other forms of life to exist on different vibrations. I am regarded doubtfully and a little sadly for a moment, and the conversation is promptly changed to more mundane matters. But since I can accept the verity of ghosts without difficulty, I am myself unable to understand why I cannot accept the existence of water horses. It is a pity, for apparently they abound up here.

The water horse's head is shaped like that of a horse, but its ears are shorter and its neck longer. It frequents lochs and has a disconcerting habit of appearing on land in the guise of a horse. Should anyone mount it while it is on land it will make for its natural element where, assuming its true form, it will disappear beneath the surface with the luckless rider. Water horses have been known to take other shapes when on land, besides that of horses. On the whole, their reputation is none too good. In the past many deaths by drowning were attributed to them. They have touchy natures and are quick to take offence at any fancied slight, wreaking swift and ruthless vengeance on the miscreant. For failing to bid a water horse good-day, for instance, the person guilty of such boorish manners may be lured towards a loch on some pretext by the offended creature, and there dragged beneath the waters.

Mr. Fraser, who had seen and talked to several and could never understand my disbelief in their existence, knew of a man who had met one in the shape of a cow as it was grazing in his croft garden. Not unnaturally, he flung a stone at it, calling it several uncomplimentary things as he did so. The stone found its mark and the cow—to the man's dismay—uttered a loud whinny of distress. A whinny coming from a cow could only mean that the creature was in fact a water horse. He then noticed that, unlike a cow, it had short round ears. Although he was quick to shout an apology the harm was done; the water horse had taken dire offence. Without ado, it trotted up to him, seized him by the collar and started to drag him towards a nearby loch. His wife meantime, having seen what was happening, seized a dish of brose and hurried along after them. As her spouse was being dragged by the collar into the loch she held out the dish and requested the water horse to come and eat it. When I heard this tale for the first time I was surprised to learn that the offer was accepted. The water horse promptly let go of the man and proceeded to tuck into the brose. Having once sampled brose myself, I felt that the water horse's culinary taste was not of a particularly high order.

Occasionally, if treated with deference, these creatures put themselves out to be helpful to man. Mr. Fraser's father used to be on uncommonly good terms with one who, whenever he whistled, would swim towards him across the loch and carry him on its back to the other side. Small rewards in the shape of provender and an occasional nip of whisky were, of course, expected in return for this service.

"I wouldn't put Mr. Fraser's father past taking a few nips himself," Aunt Miriam remarked when I told her about the friendly water horse.

For myself, I think that seals may be responsible for starting the water horse myth, just as they started the mermaid legends among mariners. Common seals frequently swim quite long distances down rivers, and have been known to spend days in inland lochs.

Whenever Mr. Fraser was working on a spell he took care to do the actual casting during the evening. I asked him if this was the most propitious time.

"It's the best time for me to work at a spell nowadays," he replied. "That's when my strength is greatest, d'ye see? When I first started to practise what I had learnt from my mother I was little more than a boy. Then I did the important work in the mornings. In my middle years it was the afternoon, and now it is the evening."

He went on to say that according to old Celtic occult lore we belong in the morning of our lives, or childhood, to the sea; in the afternoon, or maturity, to the land; and in the evening, or old age, to the air. Only after death do we mingle with and belong to all three elements. Then Time is undifferentiated, like a great wave which never breaks, like a wind blowing strong and free forever, like a vast range of hills unbroken by any plain. In this eternal time our strength does not ebb or flow and no moment is more propitious than another.

According to the wise one's age, he will call upon the relevant spirits of sea, land, or air to abet him. During youth, water will be much used in casting spells and making up potions; later a pinch of earth. In old age the ceremonies are performed under the dome of the Wind Weaver (Norse for sky). And also to be considered is the person or animal for whom the spell is to be cast. In Scotland, as in most other countries, the female sex is symbolised by water, and the male by fire. In the old days every bird, beast, fish and plant familiar to the district—and even some of the rarer visitors—had its particular place in the mystic world and its mystic attributes, all of which the wise one had to know. As nothing lives unto itself, it followed that each species reacted favourably, neutrally or adversely upon other forms of life. A curlew's mystic family characteristics might be annotated as follows: spirit—air (as like all birds); gender of the species—female (water); effective as an aid in the curing of brain diseases and restoring failing mental energy. It is a bird associated with death, although this by no means made it a bird of ill omen. On the contrary, the cry of a curlew when someone was dying was considered auspicious, for this lonely yet somehow beautiful cry was thought to aid the soul to leave the body, and make easy its passing into the other world.

Wise men and women were also called 'links'. The bird, plant and animal kingdoms also had their links, albeit unconscious ones. A bat is the link between air and earth; the rowan tree between plant and man; and the seal—a creature of considerable mystic significance—the link between sea and land, the sea creatures and man. Here is a seal story related to me by Mr. Fraser, which tells of the result of selfish love and of the seal's mystic powers.

There was a woman of Wester Ross who lived alone in a croft down by the shore. The croft was on a stretch of green machair (the grass growing between the land and beach). Every day she would collect driftwood and dulse (a red edible seaweed) and sing to herself as she walked over the white sands. When she stopped singing she would listen to the waves and say to herself, "If only I could understand the voice of the ocean then I would be a wise woman indeed." But she had not the gift. One night when there was a *gealach fhoghair* (harvest moon) in the sky the waves rose up high like horses and beat upon the sand. But although she heard clearly the crash and boom she could not hear the inner speech, for she had not the gift. Then far out to sea in the ring of the yellow moon lying upon a rock she saw a seal. She went down to the beach and the tongues of the waves swept over her bare feet.

As loud as she was able, she called, "O seal, if you can swim in these high seas, swim over to me here." And from where she was standing she heard the seal laugh as it plunged fearlessly into the ocean.

"I am a young she-seal," it said as it swum up to her, "and I can swim among the great Atlantic rollers as easily as you can walk among the hills. Why did you call me?"

"Come live wie me a while in my croft," said the woman. "I will treat you as though you were my own daughter. Have no fear that I will keep you frae the ocean. You will tell me what the waves speak of, for it is given to seals to understand the voice of the ocean and the land."

The seal nodded.

So the seal went to live with the woman in her croft. In the evenings they would sit by the peat fire drinking tea and eating girdle cakes and in the mornings they would walk together over the sands.

"What are the waves saying?" the woman would ask.

The seal would listen a moment then say, "Now they are speaking of the shoals of herrings swimming off the shore."

"Go catch me some," the woman would bid, and dutifully the seal would swim off and return later with a mouth full of herrings.

Through the seal, she came to know of what was going on in the ocean and though she lived far from the nearest clachan her fame as a wise woman began to spread fast. Fishermen came to ask her advice about the tides and when there was a likelihood of shoals of fish approaching the shore. The woman was happy to earn this reputation. She grew very attached to the seal and treated it indeed as if it were her own daughter.

Then one day as the seal was swimming in the waves it met with a he-seal.

"Swim awa' wie me and be my mate," it said.

As they plunged and dived together through the rollers the she-seal knew for a certainty that she had found her mate and the time had come for her to leave her human companion.

"Let us swim awa' together now."

"First I must speak to the woman who lives in that distant croft and tell her of my intention, for during these past months she has been like a mother to me."

They swam to the shore.

"The time has come for me to leave the croft and live in the ocean, human mother. Today, swimming in the waves, I found my seal mate."

"He's awfu' plain," was all the woman said, though to herself she muttered, "Faithless one to think of leaving me after all the kindness I have lavished on you."

"I won't be forgetting you," the seal continued. "When the moon is full I will return wie my mate and tell you the secrets of the ocean as before. And now he and I must swim awa'."

"Spend one more night wie me," the woman begged. "You cannot grudge me that."

To this the seal agreed. She told her mate she would wait for him on the rock the following morning.

Directly the seal fell asleep that night the woman started to weave a long, narrow length of material from a strong yarn. Before light broke she fastened one end of it round the seal's neck, making it captive.

"You shall not leave me," she told it. "Each day you may swim in the ocean at the end of this rope so that you can tell me what is happening in the deeps and you may speak to your mate if you wish. But I will keep you fast on the rope all the while."

The seal cried bitterly and pleaded with the woman to let her go free. To no avail.

Each day she swam in the ocean at the end of the rope and each day her mate waited for her on the rock. Jealous as the woman was as she watched them speaking together she let them be because she wanted to know all that was going on in the ocean.

The *gealach fhoghair* rose again. The seal looked from a croft window and saw its mate sitting on the rock, a dark speck in the yellow globe. The waves rose up high like horses and crashed upon the sand.

"Let me go to him for a wee while," she pleaded.

The woman consented to this request, keeping fast to the end of the rope as the seal swam out to its mate.

They talked together for several minutes and then as she felt the rope jerk for her return, she cried, "The moon and the waves are bidding me swim far awa' with you across the ocean."

She plunged into the tossing waves and strained and twisted against the rope, trying to free herself. As her struggles grew more frantic, the knot slipped and the rope tightened round her neck like a noose.

"She struggles against me," said the woman, pulling it in.

As she hauled in the last length of rope she saw to her dismay that the seal was dead.

Its mate came and wept by the lifeless body. "I will never find another mate like her. Single I will remain to the end of my days." Then it lifted up its head and listened. "Between the crash of the waves I can hear her voice. Her spirit will return to me when I lie dying." And it swam off and soon disappeared among the rollers.

In the years which followed the woman lost her reputation as a wise one, for without the seal her power was gone. Loneliness and unease possessed her. When the wind keened drearily it made her grue (shiver).

"Her spirit will come and take revenge on mine when death is looming," she thought. This fear grew strong within her so that she dreaded the sinking of the sun each evening which brought death a day nearer.

She became mortally ill, a fever gripped her one night and wracked her body. But in spite of her weakened state she could not remain on her bed. An increasing fear and restlessness of spirit drove her from the croft in the early hours of the morning. As she staggered across the sands she saw a dark shadow on the sea which drew ever closer to the shore.

"Do not come to torture me," she cried out in terror—"I have paid for my selfishness and more these past years."

But the dark shadow moved steadily shorewards. When it emerged from the waves she saw that it was the he-seal. The hair on its throat was as white as the hair on her head, and its eyes were dimmed by old age and approaching death. She fell down on the sand and the seal came and lay down beside her.

"I hae been alane a long while," it said. "But soon now she will come to me."

As Death drew the spirit from the woman's nostrils, her eyes were opened to both worlds and she saw the ghost of the she-seal coming towards her. But it paid her no heed; it looked only at its dying mate. When the seal's spirit had emerged from its body the two went off together into the endless reaches of eternity. True love seeks no revenge.

Fear left the woman. For a few seconds as her spirit fluttered between life and death, she was able to understand the voice of the ocean. As the waves rose and fell they sang, "Alone…"

"For eternity?"

"Alone…" they answered.

The voice of the ocean faded.

As the woman looked about her in vain for the seal spirits she knew a sadness that struck deeper than any fear.

It was from Mr. Fraser that I first heard what is perhaps the most beautiful and best known of all Celtic stories—the Children of Lir. This story, like many of the old Celtic tales, is symbolic of the passing of the country from paganism to Christianity. For those who do not know it let me quote it briefly.

There was a king named Lir who lived in the Land of Youth. His castle was a magnificent building surrounded by tall trees. He and his wife had four children. The eldest child was a girl named Fionuala. The three boys were named Conn, Fiachra and Hugh. These children were all of exceptional grace and beauty and were much loved by their parents. When they were still young the Queen died and King Lir married her sister, a woman named Aoife (pronounced Eefa).

Because of the King's great love for his children she grew exceedingly jealous of them and her jealousy had a bitterness to it as she herself remained childless. She resolved their destruction.

To this end, she decided to go on a journey to a neighbouring king named Bov, taking the children with her. The children bade their father good-bye and set off with the Queen. They journeyed over moors and through forests and eventually came to a lonely spot near Lake Derryvaragh. Here Queen Aoife ordered her attendants to kill the children. This they refused to do so she resolved to do the deed herself, but her womanhood overcame her and instead of killing them she transformed them into four white swans, laying on them the following curse: three hundred years they must spend on the waters of Lake Derryvaragh; three hundred years on the Straits of Moyle which lie between Scotland and Ireland; three hundred years on the Atlantic by Erris and Inishglory. After which time, when the Woman of the South is betrothed to the Man of the North, the enchantment will end.

When Queen Aoife arrived at the castle of King Bov without the children her guilt was discovered and he changed her into a demon of the air. With a wild screech, she flew over the castle and was never seen again.

Heartbroken, King Lir went out with King Bov to seek the

swan children. Eventually they found them on the shores of
Lake Derryvaragh. To the father's joy, they could still speak the
human tongue and, moreover, were able to make wonderful
music. People came from many miles to converse with them
and listen to their music. Throughout this period peace and
harmony pervaded the land.

The time came for them to depart for the Straits of Moyle
where the seas continually toss and winds rip the sails of the
ships. Here they underwent the worst of their sufferings. Cut
off from humankind, they endured loneliness, cold and storm.
During winter nights their feathers often froze to the rocks and
they were sometimes driven apart by storms. Fionuala, always
the leader, would wrap her plumage round the youngest swan
and the four of them would sit close in an endeavour to ward
off the chill. As they sat shivering, Fionuala would sing them
this song:

> Our stepmother's heart was cruel,
> She used her magic ill,
> Driving us out on the raging sea,
> Four white swans who once were mortal.
>
> Our bath is the frothing brine,
> In bays by red rocks guarded,
> For mead at our father's table
> We drink of the salt, blue water.
>
> Three sons and a single daughter
> In clefts of the cold rocks dwelling,
> The hard rocks cruel as Aoife—
> We are full of keening tonight.

They took flight to the western shores of Mayo for the last period of their enchantment. A young farmer discovered who they were and befriended them. To him they told their story and he it was who handed it down.

Eventually they returned to their father's castle in the Land of Youth, but although it was still standing they were unable to find it. Their eyes had been sealed because they had a higher destiny.

On Erris Bay they heard for the first time the sound of a Christian bell coming from the chapel of a hermit. The thin, dreadful sound terrified the swans but the hermit managed to overcome their fears and instructed them in the Christian faith. Every day, to the delight of the people living round about, they joined in the singing in the chapel.

Now it happened that a Princess Deoca, the Woman of the South, became betrothed to the Man of the North who was a chief named Lairgnen. She asked him to give her the four wonderful singing swans as a wedding present. But the priest refused to part with them. So Lairgnen dragged them off forcibly by the silver chains with which the priest had coupled them, and took them to Deoca. This was to be their last trial.

In the presence of these two, the Man from the North and the Woman from the South, their swan plumage fell away and they became four withered, decrepit, white-haired human beings of a vast old age. Lairgnen and Deoca fled from them in horror. The hermit realising that their end was near, baptised them immediately.

"Lay us in one grave," said Fionuala, "and place Conn at my right hand and Fiachra at my left and Hugh before my face, for there they were wont to be when I sheltered them through many a winter's night upon the seas of Moyle."

This was done. Their spirits ascended heavenwards. But the hermit, so the tale goes, sorrowed for them to the end of his earthly days.

As will be realised after reading these two tales, magic—which could be used both for good or evil purposes—was once an integral part of life.

In Wester Ross some years back I spent a few days with an old woman who was reputed to have the gift of seeing visions. She had foretold many local events and happenings to various individuals, seeing them with her inner eye. Should a person about whom she had had a vision be slightly psychic himself she would tell him to put a hand on her shoulder, a foot on her foot and then look into her eyes so that he might see the vision for himself. Apparently she could conjure up a vision again after having seen it and project it to another sensitive, somewhat in the same manner as a person gives a cinematograph display by turning the handle of the projector.

"Have you had any vision concerning me?" I asked her.

"Aye," she replied.

"Then let me try and see it for myself."

"There's not many who can see visions for themselves these days."

Nevertheless I made an attempt to get a preview of what was going to befall me at some future date, placing a hand on her shoulder and a foot on her foot as she instructed.

"Do you see aught?"

My eyes strayed from hers to a photograph hanging on the wall of a rather fearsome male, sporting a tartan tammie set at a defiant angle and a huge pair of walrus moustaches, the ends of which were waxed to a fine point. His frown, so different from the unctuous smiles prevalent in most photographs, would, I felt certain, make even the most self-assured individual a trifle apprehensive.

"I see naught," I answered somewhat guiltily, glancing away.

"I will hae to tell you then."

"Who is that?" I asked.

My hostess looked in the direction I indicated.

"That's Uncle Garry. He became a minister o' the kirk, but that did not stop him swinging his golf clubs on the Sabbath. Aye, and never a word did the folks say agin him though observance is strict in these parts."

Quite. I consoled myself that what I lacked in psychic perception I made up for in acute judgement of character from a person's features.

"The vision I hae o' you is a bit uncomfortable. You are hanging upside down, d'you see? Over on your right side is a strong twisty branch which you would do well to try and clutch when the vision comes to pass. There is naught more I can see than that."

This was not quite the kind of vision I had hoped for, and not being one to practise acrobatics I put it from my mind. Eighteen months later, when I was staying at the house of a relative, I was laying out a hairbrush and comb on the windowsill to dry when something caught my attention in the flower bed below. I leaned right over the sill to get a better look and fell out. A large thickly-leaved pear tree grew up to the first floor windows and as I hit it I promptly remembered the vision. Automatically I turned my head to the right and saw a strong twisty branch. The tree supported my weight for a space during which I made frantic efforts to grab hold of the branch, but I failed to do so. I descended head first down the length of the pear tree to the sound of snapping twigs and landed with an exceedingly

uncomfortable bump on to the flower bed. Later, while liberally applying ointment and adhesive plaster to the injuries, I
had to admit that the vision had been correct in every detail.
Nowadays I refuse adamantly to have anything to do with fore-
telling of the future. The most unlikely looking gipsies at charity
bazaars, arrayed in brass ear-rings, embroidered blouses and
dirndl skirts, have me heading in the opposite direction when
they offer to tell my fortune for two shillings. I prefer to remain
in ignorance as to what the future holds in store for me.

"Could I hae the company of Lora a while to help wie a spell?"
Mr. Fraser asked me one day.

He had walked over to us accompanied by an old crofter
whose new cow, young and bought only two weeks back with
a little pile of money he and his wife had saved, was seriously
ill. He had informed Mr. Fraser—to the latter's pleasure—that
he was not going to have any vet tampering with her.

We went down to the lochan. Repeated calls did not bring
Lora to the shore so I returned to the croft for the trumpet.
Although I blew several strong blasts they also had no effect.
Hansel and Gretel arrived on the scene in answer to the sum-
mons, but as Mr. Fraser pointed out, otters did not have the
mystic power of seals. We stood about in the hope she would
appear. I felt very reluctant to let the old crofter go back without
the spell for his cow having the added benefit of Lora's mystic
power. In all, his walk to and from his home would total close on
thirty miles. Then, to my annoyance, I saw Lora lying a few yards
away between two rocks—her favourite resting place—eyeing
us placidly but making no attempt to stir herself and come
over. She wiped her nose with a flexible fore-flipper and stood
almost erect as she surveyed the countryside. At last she swam
across the inlet.

Mr. Fraser asked the crofter and me to stand a short distance away. He opened a tin box in which were some herbs and what appeared to be a lump of clayey substance.

As he worked the herbs into the clay ball he held it under Lora's nose. Then he spoke to her earnestly a minute and put the herbal ball back into the tin. Beckoning us over, he handed the tin to the crofter, telling him to administer the ball to the sick animal directly he got home, and on the following morning to give it a pint of 'straight medicine' made up according to his instructions. He informed us that it was Lora's breath that lent such a vital quality to the spell; he had also asked her co-operation for its success.

I am happy to be able to report that the cow eventually recovered and lived to a ripe old age. But whether recovery was due to the spell or the straight medicine or to both—I am not sufficiently qualified either in spell-making or medicine to be able to proffer an opinion.

seal watching

Five years of croft life had wrought certain changes in us. We seldom glanced at the parlour clock unless to note whether it was time to listen to the news or to a particular programme. About the only other occasions we checked on the time was before starting off on a trip to the township or clachan. The weather and seasons regulated our working day, our rising and retiring. Living apart from a community and being as nearly self-contained as is possible in these islands, we often found it hard to counteract the feeling that we were in a separate domain inhabited so far as humanity was concerned solely by ourselves, Mr. McNairn and the Frasers. Events in Glasgow or London seemed as remote to us as happenings in Calcutta. I was perfectly content to go on living thus, and as the years passed I found it more and more of an effort to take a reasonable interest in outside news. My only concern during this period of my life was that I should fail to pass an educational test—to undertake which I journeyed occasionally to Edinburgh—and be compelled by the authorities to go to a boarding school. In order to avoid this unpleasant possibility I worked diligently at my lessons and miraculously never failed a test. Every so often Aunt Miriam would suggest that I spend a week or so staying with young cousins and their families, whereupon I would promptly suggest that they came to us instead. This they were always eager to do whereas I, for my part, was always extremely reluctant to leave home even for a few days.

During these five years the two gardens had improved considerably. Although we had been told by more experienced gardeners than ourselves that tomatoes would never grow up here, or that if they did they would remain green, the ones we planted generally reached a fair size and ripened well. In a good season we had enough over to bottle. Of course, fruit and plants are usually two weeks behind those grown farther south, for spring starts late and winter sets in early. Marrows in the lochan garden did not do too badly either, and stuffed marrow became a frequent item on the summer menu.

Our animals had all done well during this period. Like ourselves, they had not one of them suffered a single illness. Rodney, between his second and fifth year, filled out a lot. When a friend and her miniature dachshund came to stay there was little difference between its weight and size and that of Rodney, though the dog stood higher than he did. The first thing Rodney did on meeting this canine visitor was to give it a sharp nip on the leg. The dog, a most docile creature which had done nothing to provoke him, thereafter bolted whenever Rodney approached him.

It surprised us that the otters had remained with us so long. They wandered off for days at a time but always returned sooner or later. One of their holts (an otter's lair) was under a rock near the lochan. Here they would retire for hours, coming up if I called them. I always hoped that they would produce a young one not too far from the croft, so that I could study its upbringing. But this was not to be. In their fifth year they wandered off on one of their frequent excursions. A week passed and still they did not return. I visited the holt but there was no sign that they had been back to it since leaving. When three weeks had gone by and they were still away I reconciled myself to the idea that they had most probably gone for good, although I could not refrain from hoping that they would return one day. The absence of these two playful creatures made a gap in my life, which the presence of a young red deer did nothing to fill. This deer ran off while it was a youngster, having proved itself, like Sith, to be a most troublesome pet.

Then one night, I awoke to hear an animal outside the croft give several low whines as though it were in great pain. Even before I was up I heard Aunt Miriam go out, and full of foreboding I followed her. Gretel was lying on the step. In the torchlight I saw that she was completely exhausted and that one of her forepaws was dreadfully torn, the lower portion being almost severed from the upper. The paw was completely crushed. Aunt carried her into the parlour and a short inspection showed that it would be useless to try and heal her. Her wounded leg apart, her condition was now so emaciated that this alone would have made recovery very doubtful. She was given an injection to end her life. Nine miles from us would have been the nearest distance in which she could have got caught in a gin trap, but it is likely that she got trapped in one a good deal farther away than this. Somehow she had managed to free her paw from its grip, and had travelled those miles back to her old home. When she left us she was five years and four months old, and weighed twenty-one pounds. Hansel weighed twenty-eight. After her death she was put on the scales and they registered nine-and-a-half pounds.

I give these details to show the terrible cruelty involved in using this most merciless method of destroying animals. Since

1934 the possibility of banning the gin trap has been brought up in Parliament five times and turned down. Nineteen fifty-four saw a law passed which will in all probability make the gin trap illegal, as from the year 1958. Those who have the welfare of animals at heart can only hope that this will at last come into being and that the gin trap will be abolished for good.

The following morning Hansel appeared. He hurried over to the croft and sniffed at the step where Gretel had lain the previous night. Then he went through all the rooms. As if finally realising that to search any farther was useless, he went out again. I made him up a plate of bread, milk and oil, which he ate. For the rest of the day he wandered in the vicinity of the croft. Then in the evening he departed and that was the last we ever saw of him. Otters, I may remark in passing, become very attached to one another and frequently mate for life.

After Gretel's death I felt a sudden desire to get away from the croft for a while. With Aunt Miriam's permission, I started to plan a trip which I had often contemplated since our arrival. This would take me through that desolate stretch of country which continued almost unbroken from the door of our croft northwards to the mouth of the Strathy, a distance of some thirty miles. A good road crosses this country midway from Kinbrace to the Naver valley, north of which roadways and accommodation are virtually non-existent. Not wishing to walk as far east as Kinbrace, where it would have been possible to replenish supplies, I took enough food with me to last a maximum of five days, by which time I reckoned to reach the coast. Food consisted of two loaves, fat, a packet of dehydrated potatoes, a packet of dried bananas, tea, and a tin of condensed milk with which to make the essential cups of tea. Berries and dandelion leaves I would be able to gather en route to supply vitamin needs, and I hoped to be able to buy an occasional egg

and glass of fresh milk from a crofter. My camping kit consisted
of a light silk, waterproofed tent, sleeping bag, saucepan, fry-
ing-pan, primus, matches, compass and map. I also took with
me the bamboo pipe with which to amuse myself during the
evenings.

The first part of my route took me along the River Skinsdale
and up through the Borrobol Forest. From there I headed due
north until I came to the road. The three big lochs—Baddanloch, Chlair and nan Cuinne which run into each other—lay
over to my left. I crossed the road and entered the country
which I had come to explore. That first night in new territory
I spent encamped in a birch spinney close to Loch Leum a
Chlamhain, with Ben Griam Beg rising behind me. This large
hill, hardly big enough to be called a mountain, is typical of
many in Sutherland which rise to 1,000 or 1,500 feet, and whose
slopes are composed of grass and loose scree. They offer no
challenge to the mountaineer but are well worth climbing for
the surrounding view they offer of the countryside.

During the evening I cooked my main meal of the day, a not
very exciting repast consisting of mashed potato and butter,
a slice of bread, a few bananas and two cups of tea, as well as
berries and edible greenstuffs I had picked during the day. As
I was eating supper and idly watching a grouse in flight I saw
it suddenly snatched up in the talons of a golden eagle. I had
twice before seen this great bird (the female of the species is
a few inches larger than the male) swoop on prey lying on the
ground, but I had never before seen it catch prey in the air.
At this campsite I also found a young water shrew under my
sleeping bag when I lifted it up on the following morning. The
shrew hurried off lochwards, no doubt to search for grubs in
order to satisfy its voracious appetite. Breakfast was a cup of tea
and slice of bread-and-butter. This diet of a light breakfast and

a solid supper with nothing taken in between, except perhaps for a handful of berries, I have found to be adequate on short trips of this sort.

The country swept onwards, hill succeeding hill. Streams ran between clumps of dwarf willow, and under rocks which stood like prehistoric monsters on the skyline. On my third day's walk the land grew flatter and I was able to see far into the distance. At the northern end of Loch nam Breach I started to follow the Uair which runs into it and is a tributary of Strathy Water. From now on I increased my pace; a few dried bananas and half a loaf, which had hardened to rusk-like consistency, were all that was left of my food supply. At the junction of the Uair and Strathy Water I came across a track which I followed for the rest of the way. For three days I had not seen a single person and had only once glimpsed far off the white walls of a lonely croft. On the fifth day I reached the mouth of Strathy Water. That evening I pitched my tent near the region of Strathy Bay.

Here, surrounded by eggs, rashers of bacon, a can of milk, butter, and a loaf of bread purchased from a crofter woman, I was just starting eagerly to prepare a really good supper when I saw a Common Seal resting on a rock a little way out to sea. The sight of it lying there watching me warily, gave me an idea and I drew the bamboo pipe from my rucksack. Its uneasiness seemed to increase and for a moment I thought it was going to dive straightway off the rock. I quickly piped a few notes and the seal raised its head and listened. For a while I continued to pipe and the seal, though I could tell it was engrossed by the sounds, nevertheless continued to watch me uneasily. With extreme caution, and still piping away hard, I began to move across the machair on my heels in a squatting position, very slowly, an inch or so at a time, and, once over the bright green machair, onwards down the beach. Several times during these uncomfortable manoeuvres the seal's body jerked and it glanced down at the calm waters as though it had decided that, music or no music, the time had come to plunge in. During these moments I froze and piped several high and—I hoped—enticing notes of the kind which invariably sent Lora off into one of her trance-like states. The trick worked and I was able to reach the fringe of the sea without my quarry, now only some five yards distant, leaving its rock. Then I lost my balance and sat down with a splash in the foam, and the seal immediately plunged into the shallow water and made out to sea. It took me several minutes to straighten out my cramped limbs again.

The next morning the seal was back, sunning itself on the rock. Remembering my uncomfortable progress of the day before, this time I approached it upright. It listened intently to the piping and I was able to get within about eight feet of it. The creature was a well developed male. As I studied it the sun shone almost directly on to its large eyes and they appeared a clear brilliant orange. I did not attempt to get any closer and started to back away again. Its eyes never left me until I was well up the beach, then it relaxed and turned over on its side, enjoying the sunshine. When I left the beach it was lying on its back, its head hanging over the rock in an attitude of complete repose. Resting seals seem to favour this attitude. Both outside and in the croft Lora would often lie stretched out full length on her back with her flippers hanging limp at her sides and her eyes closed.

Later I went on another trip for the purpose of studying seals in their wild state, and this took me up to the Shetland Isles. Round their shores are to be found the largest numbers of Common Seals in Britain. Groups numbering between forty and fifty are not uncommon.

The Common Seal has its pup in June. Birth usually takes place on a rock or skerry, the pup following its mother into the sea on the same day. The little creature's coat is almost identical with that of an adult seal except that it is more vividly spotted.

I once came across a very young seal, perhaps a few hours' old, with its mother. She left it lying on a rock while she went off for a short swim. When she returned she lay down on the rock beside the pup and shortly after this the two went into the sea together, the young one following its parent without any apparent reluctance. The pup kept up well with the adult. I watched them through my field glasses as they swam to another rock a little farther inland.

I managed to get on quite good acquaintanceship with this lone pair, who frequented this strip of coastline. Sometimes the pup would remain on a rock or the beach while the mother went off for a swim by herself. Whenever this happened I approached the young seal and played a tune on the pipe. It soon became used to seeing me about and would look up with an alert expression whenever it heard the piping. If the parent was with it I took care to keep a certain distance and to assume an attitude of complete indifference towards her and the pup. After a while, though, she too became used to seeing me about, and as long as I did not approach too close she would suckle her offspring and play with it while I sat watching at some vantage point. Some of my happiest memories of seals are of these two. Like most highly developed mammals, they played together with evident enjoyment and the mother's care of the youngster was admirable.

One day when the tide was out, the two played together in the surf, the mother rolling the rotund pup down a short distance of beach and into the wavelets. Another favourite game was chasing each other in the sea in much the same way as dogs will chase each other on land. When I was on the beach one day I saw the pup sitting alone by a rock pool watching me. I went and picked it up. Immediately it started to make a distressed baaing sound, reminiscent of a sheep, while at the same time large tears rolled down its face. Not wishing to be the cause of so much distress, I returned it to the rock on which it had been sitting. As I walked away, perversely it began to waddle after me. I prised a mussel off a rock with a penknife I carried, extracted the meat and offered it to the seal. The offering was refused but confidence having been once more established, I held out the bamboo pipe which it took in its mouth, dropped and picked up again. For a while I played with it, holding on to the pipe which it tugged hard, uttering grunts of enjoyment.

Seals have an acute sense of smell, and not knowing how the mother would act towards it if she smelt that it had been handled on her return, I lifted it up and sat it in a pool, splashing water liberally over its head and body.

It protested with grunts at this treatment but showed no signs of fear.

That same summer I again visited a seal colony in the Shetlands. Although I stayed over a week and invariably approached the colony with extreme caution walking up wind, hiding behind rocks, or, when there were no rocks, propelling myself along full length on my stomach a few feet at a time, I nevertheless seldom managed to get within a hundred yards without adults and young plunging into the sea. Most of the time I had to be content with watching them through the field glasses. Young seals often climb on to their mothers' backs as they swim, and thus get a free ride. Through the field glasses, I saw a seal with a youngster on its back swim lazily to the shore and lie in the surf, the pup still perched on its parent's back, both apparently enjoying the sensation of the waves which ebbed and broke over them.

The Atlantic or Grey Seal is polygamous and a more gregarious creature than the Common Seal. There is considerable difference in the breeding habits of the two species. The female Atlantic Seal gives birth to its young in late September, October, or November, when the seas are running high and storms make it impossible to reach many of the lonely islands of the Outer Hebrides. The pup is born some distance from the sea and is almost helpless for several weeks after birth. The mother remains with it constantly, living, it is believed, on her own accumulation of fat during this period. The pup retains its silky white coat for two to three weeks. When it is three weeks old it follows its mother into the sea with reluctance and from then on she ceases to pay it much attention. Although the storms which lash the islands during the breeding season do much to protect the young seal from its chief enemy, man, they also take a toll of pups each year. During a pup's early period on land there is also the danger that a bull may tread on it. Fights are frequent occurrences between bulls; each has its harem and strip of territory which it vigorously defends.

It had long been an ambition of mine to rear an Atlantic Seal pup and thus have the chance of being able to compare its habits with that of the Common Seal. It was whilst I was on Berneray that this ambition was realised. One day I found four pups, all of which were still in their white natal coats. Two, washed up on the beach, were already dead. The other two, one of which I discovered lying on a low, rocky ledge, were alive though weakly. These I carried back to the homestead in which I was staying. The female pup died that same evening. The other, a male which I called Bernie, remained in a precarious condition for several days then rallied a little. I put him on the diet of milk and oil on which I had reared Lora.

The homeward journey across the Minch was one of the worst I have ever experienced. It takes a very heavy sea indeed to prevent the boat leaving port for, needless to say, the men who man her are among the most expert of seamen.

"Aye, there's a bit of a swell. But there's nae need to fret yourself that we won't be leaving," one of the hands replied in answer to my anxious enquiry as to whether there was a likelihood of the voyage being cancelled until calmer weather prevailed. His answer was not what I had hoped for. With Bernie under an arm and a suitcase clutched in one hand I mounted the gangway with the rest of the passengers, all of whom, I noticed, had assumed expressions of stoic indifference or a repellent cheerfulness.

Soon after the little MacBrayne steamer had left Lochmaddy in North Uist, all passengers were ordered below deck. The wisest, of course, had made for the nether regions directly they had boarded the boat. Within a few minutes of setting sail my hair had been drenched with flying spray as I sat against a vent pipe, wondering mournfully whether I would be able to retain my hitherto unbroken record of good seamanship. The huge waves, of a dark grey-green colour, reminded me of nothing so much as some of the loftier hills in Sutherland. I was endeavouring to concentrate on comparisons such as these in an effort to take my mind off my squeamish inside when the order came to go below deck. As I traced a zigzag course towards the doorway the boat seemed to pause for a moment before shooting down a mountainous wave, and as it did so Bernie fell from under my arm and rotated rapidly to the far end of the deck. He was saved by one of the seamen just before going under the rails at the boat-edge.

"Tha' will do the wee beast nae guid," an old woman informed me unnecessarily, as she was half carried over the threshold by a posse of male relatives.

Downstairs, casualties were already stretched abjectly on every chair and couch. Groans from adult sufferers and wails from children rent the air. A kindly woman sitting up against a wall with her husband offered me a cushion on to which I promptly sagged. Waves smacked continuously against the portholes and the boat rolled and shuddered.

"If ye've nae objection I'll carry on recitin'," the woman said. "It's the best way I ken for taking your mind off ye plight."

By this time I was past objecting to anything. The Celt, in my opinion, suffers from few inhibitions and seldom a trace of shyness. The woman started to recite 'The Charge of the Light Brigade' by Tennyson, in a loud swinging Celtic voice, accompanied at intervals by her husband who was in a worse state than herself. No one took the slightest notice. As the poem proceeded it struck me as being singularly appropriate for the occasion.

"'Forrard the Light Brigade, charge for the guns,' she said—"

" 'He said…'"

"Will ye stop arguing wie me, Hugh,"—she said. "'Into the valley o' death rode the six hundred…' Can ye remember the next bit?" she asked, giving her husband a dig with her elbow.

"Nae. I'll be leaven' ye for a while now," he said, getting up and proceeding to wend his way unsteadily between the recumbent forms in the direction of the cloakroom.

"Nae gie in so easy, Hugh," she shouted after him. Then turning to me, she asked, "Wha's that ye're holding on your lap?"

"A seal," I murmured.

She proceeded to delve into a string bag and brought out a thermos flask, a packet of sandwiches and half a fruit cake.

"I'm nae feelin' guid, mind ye, but it doesn't make one feel better for starving oneself, does it now? Hugh's agin me there, though. Never a snippet for the whole of the voyage. Wha' hae ye brought?"

I produced a thermos and a large packet of bulky sand-wiches. The rich aroma of ham and cheese which assailed my nostrils forced me to assume a full length position in order to counteract a sudden spell of giddiness. At this point, a young girl, aged about ten, who, as I had been vaguely aware, had been watching me, came over and sat by my side. In marked contrast to everyone else within sight, her cheeks were a bright pink and she appeared to be in the best of spirits.

"Ye'll nae be lasting out much longer—I'll look after him for ye," and she picked up Bernie from my side. "Would ye like me to take the sandwiches too?"

"Please."

"It's a pity to waste them. I've eaten ours but I could still do wie another bite. Will ye be wanting?…"

"Take it," I said, pushing the thermos towards her.

The woman leaned across me. "Can ye think of a poem ?"

"Aye," the girl replied promptly, adjusting Bernie's rug about his neck.

> " 'Wee, sleekit, cowrin', tim'rous beastie,
> Oh, wha' a panic's in thy breastie,
> Thou need nae—' "

"Guid. Let me say the next bit. *'Thou need nae start awa' sae hasty...'* "

To the sound of a Burns' poem and slapping waves I faded out of the picture for the rest of the voyage.

On arrival home I promised my long-suffering Aunt that

Bernie would definitely be taken to the sea directly he was able to fend for himself.

The Atlantic Seal, though the larger of the two species, has a smaller brain-pan and consequently is the less intelligent and lively. Owing to Bernie's continued weakly condition I was not able to compare him too closely with Lora in her pup days. There was, however, one very noticeable difference between the two seals. Unlike Lora, who as a pup had clamoured for attention and company, and who from the first had shown no objection to being handled, Bernie to the end of his short life showed a marked distaste for being picked up. Whenever I approached him he uttered grunts of protest and attempted to extricate himself from my hold, whilst the tear-flow increased considerably. I experienced great difficulty in getting him to suck from the bottle. After two weeks of handling he became more tolerant of my presence, although not once was I greeted after an absence with any display of pleasure.

Lora's reaction towards him was curious. Till his arrival she had never before evinced the slightest trace of jealousy towards another mammal. If Aunt Miriam or myself stroked an otter on our lap Lora showed no concern that she was not receiving attention also. From the first day of Bernie's arrival, however, it became obvious that she had taken a violent dislike to him. If one of us took Bernie on our laps in her presence she started to bark furiously and raised herself almost upright on her tail in an attempt to snap at him. We dared not leave the two of them together for fear of Lora doing her fellow seal serious harm.

When Bernie was in the region of four to five weeks old and had lost his white natal coat I decided that as his health had improved somewhat a short swim in the lochan might add to his wellbeing. I took him out in the rowboat and, keeping to fairly shallow water, dropped him in. He was swimming well and following the boat back to the shore, when Lora, who unnoticed by me, had been dozing close by on a rock, dived off and in a few seconds had overtaken the youngster. There followed a most unpleasant scene in which Lora pulled the luckless Bernie under the water by his hind flippers and I, helpless in the boat, could only wait anxiously for their reappearance. As the water was shallow it was not long before they surfaced some yards ahead of the boat. Lora still had the young seal gripped firmly by the tail and next proceeded to shake him hard, while poor Bernie, having recovered his breath, uttered piteous wails. I rowed quickly towards them and managed to catch Lora a wallop with an oar. But this did not have the effect of making her drop Bernie. Once more she dived, this time right under the boat, almost upsetting it owing to the shallowness of the water. I waited with an oar poised. When the pair surfaced again I was able to reach her and bestow several hard whacks whilst she, balanced in the water on her tail, recommenced the shaking, which now—ominously—Bernie endured without so much as a moan. At last she dropped him and I was able to pull him into the boat with the aid of an oar before he sank. As the old woman in the steamer would have said, the combined ducking and trouncing "did the wee beast nae guid" and from that hour Bernie's condition worsened rapidly and he died two days later, having been with me just over three weeks.

wild cats and other animals

One April when the snows had vanished from the hilltops, Aunt Miriam decided to go away for a spell to friends in Argyll. I drove her down to Lairg in the trap, returning home alone with the monthly provisions. It was the first time my Aunt had been away from the croft during the six years we had lived there.

With only the animals for company, I soon discovered that—good companions though they were—I was not cut out for a hermit's existence for any lengthy period. The work around and about the croft did not prove beyond my capabilities; April on the whole is not too rigorous a month. But what I came to realise only too clearly was my own inadequate resources with which to counter a long spell of solitude. Life, I found, withered when there was no close companion at hand to discuss the small daily happenings and to share a joke. As I had no neighbours living close by to wonder whether my mind was ailing, I carried on long conversations with myself and with the animals. One particular incident which occurred when Aunt Miriam was away I found so amusing that it kept me laughing at intervals for several days. I had baked a batch of scones and had just removed them from the oven on the tin tray when one of the goats, which I had omitted to tether, walked into the parlour, snatched up a piping hot scone and promptly dropped it. She regarded me balefully for an instant, then turned and walked out in a dignified fashion.

To while away the long evening hours Lora and I had several musical soirées. This was perhaps the only period in her life when she might have suffered from an overdose of practising. Though she was never a laggard in this respect I kept her hard at it and occasionally she flung down the beater or mouth organ in exasperation. By the time Aunt Miriam returned I wanted my pet to have learnt three more tunes: 'Roses of Picardy', 'Speak to me only with thine eyes', and 'A Nightingale Sang in Berkeley Square', the first two to be played respectively on the mouth organ and xylophone, the last to be rendered vocally. It was while Lora and I were in the middle of one of these soirées that I noticed far off along the valley the flicker of a small fire against which a figure was now and then silhouetted. I suspected the arrival of tinkers, and remembering the last lot I felt a certain uneasiness at being alone in the croft.

My surmise proved to be correct. Early the following morning an old tinker came to the door and asked if I could spare him milk and bread in return for doing a job of work. This couple, an old man and his wife who were both in their eighties, were very different from the previous group of tinkers who had camped in the valley. They told me later that after many years of roaming the Scottish countryside they had at last bought a croft on the shores of Wester Ross and settled down to a semi-nomadic existence. So ingrained in their natures was the urge to wander that in spring they would set out on the road again, leaving their cat to be looked after by a neighbour until their return weeks or months later. Like most tinkers these days, they had earned their living, not by mending pots and pans, as did their ancestors, but by working in the fields doing casual labour.

They were both much taken with Lora and asked if they might supplement her solo efforts with contributions of their own, to which I readily agreed. The musical sessions were changed to the afternoons. They generally consisted of instrumental renderings by Lora, a song or two from the old woman, and a piano piece by myself. The old man invariably wound up the proceedings with a sermon. Some years back he had been converted to Christianity by a minister and, like many other converts, his zeal for the faith was unbounded. No half measures for him. No sooner was the final chord struck on the piano than he seated himself opposite the three of us and began an oration, made the more impressive by grave hieratic gestures and an occasional slap on his knee to lend emphasis to a point, which lasted as long as the rest of our efforts put together. His wife and Lora would promptly fall asleep and so it was me he earnestly entreated to mend my ways and avoid the many pitfalls of this life in order to gain heaven in the hereafter. I was spared no lurid details as to what would befall me if my footsteps erred in the paths of unrighteousness and instead of attaining heaven I should descend to the nether regions.

"Well lass, I could do wie a cup o' tea now," was the usual ending to his lengthy peroration, by which time I was very ready for one myself.

They camped in the valley for a week, helping me with the gardens and the livestock in return for food and milk, before moving southwards.

When I went to fetch Aunt Miriam I knew at once by the expression on her face—not to mention raucous miaows coming from a basket—that she too was now guilty of returning home with more fauna "I've brought them for you," she confessed, but I was not taken in by this.

The increasing din coming from the basket made me wonder whether it contained miniature tigers. In fact I was not far wrong, for it came out that my Aunt had been presented whilst on her visit with a pair of wild cat kittens.

As long as I had known her it had been an ambition of hers to possess a young specimen of this mammal. I believe I am right in saying that there is no recorded instance of one ever having been tamed, even when reared on the bottle. Secretly I think Aunt Miriam felt that, given the chance, she with her considerable power over animals might succeed where others had failed. However, the nearest she came to success was in being able eventually to approach them without being spat at.

From the moment the kits were let out of the basket they were handled with leather gloves—they were five weeks' old then—and gloves it remained during their entire sojourn with us. I still think it curious that these small beasts, which had only known their mother for a very short period, should never come to accept their human owners in the slightest degree.

The wild cat, *Felis Sylvestris* to give it its scientific name, differs quite considerably in appearance from the domestic tabby. The length of leg is longer, the tail shorter, blunted at the end and black tipped; the skull is broader. It is easily the fiercest of our larger mammals. During the two world wars their numbers have increased and they now flourish in many Scottish localities where once they were unknown.

The kits were put in a cage over in the byre and during the day this was carried out and faced with a wire run. At first they were fed from a bottle and were then put on to raw rabbit and hares' meat. No amount of handling or soft words counteracted the inborn ferocity of their natures. On picking up a kit to give it the bottle one invariably got a full set of claws in the glove. Later on, whenever a dish of meat was placed in the run we would be greeted with snarls and what I can only describe as looks of glaring hatred.

The more highly developed mammals have a strong 'play' tendency and the wild cat is no exception to this rule, playing and fondling her kits just like the domestic cat. Once, high up among the cairns in Argyll, I watched through binoculars a pair of adult cats—like otters, it is probable that the wild cat remains faithful to its mate for life; a trait very much at variance with *Felis domesticus*—which were taking it in turns to spring out at each other from behind rocks. Then they had a mock tussle on the ground, rolling over and over before one finally sped away out of sight down a corrie, closely followed by the other. Because of this trait we started to play with the kits when they were still very young, hoping that by this means they might become a little tamer. They did in fact respond to a fair extent to this treatment though not to us. Should I drag a piece of paper attached to a string in front of them they would run after it but if I bent down to stroke them their claws would come out at once and they would start to snarl and hiss.

When the cats were three months old a friend of mine came to stay, bringing with her, her ginger tabby which owing to her parents being away from home at the same time could not be left behind. This cat on its arrival was the most gentle of creatures and had led a placid existence as the family pet. But queer things were written in its karma which were eventually to manifest themselves and have a marked effect on her character.

The two wild cats were put in separate runs and, with the owner's permission, Susie was placed for a while each day with the male. At first for her own safety she was left there in a cage round which the male prowled and sniffed, sometimes giving vent to long-drawn-out, eerie yowls. His attitude gradually changed to one of indifference; he would walk about the run without giving the cage or its occupant a glance or else would stretch himself full length on top and lick his paws. Then one day when we went to collect the cage we found Susie purring happily inside and the male purring noisily on top. At the suggestion of my friend, who was as interested in the experiment as my Aunt and myself, Susie was put the following day into the run without the protection of the cage while we stood outside, leather gloved, ready to go to her rescue should she be attacked. After watching each other a moment an extraordinary performance started to take place; the two began to walk slowly round the run in follow-my-leader style, uttering meanwhile hideous yowls which were soon taken up by the female in the adjoining cage. Unable to stand the noise any longer, we left them in full chorus and retired to the croft where the din was somewhat less audible, though we remained ready to hurry back should sounds of a fight break out. When we did eventually return the two were asleep, side by side. From then on Susie spent the greater part of the day with the male who became very attached to her, moping during the periods she was removed from the run.

Her mistress left, having temporarily bequeathed Susie to us in the cause of natural science.

We kept careful watch over our temporary guest and months later we sent her owners a wire which caused considerable speculation at the local post offices. The wire, which ran as follows: *Have we your permission to mate Susie with wild male?* was answered in the affirmative.

Shortly after mating had taken place she was collected and

driven back to her home. During the latter part of her stay with us her behaviour had deteriorated; she was given to sudden fits of temper and evinced a restlessness out of keeping with her previous character. Once on stooping to pick her up I received to my dismay a scratch which extended halfway down my forearm.

We heard in due course that she had given birth to three kittens. They had the wild cat markings of black and grey stripes with black tipped tails, but their underparts and chests were a light ginger. As in all cases of crossbreeding between the wild and tame varieties, the dispositions of the kits were those of the wild cat and they proved to be as untameable as our thoroughbreds had been. When able to fend for themselves they were let loose in barren country to live according to their true natures.

Susie, the once exemplary pet, never returned to her former good behaviour, I am afraid, after her stay with us. The reports we had of her from time to time stated that she seemed continually restless and that strangers to the house had to be warned not to touch her lest they get scratched. A female cat which lived in the house next door went in terror of its life after her return as Susie promptly attacked it whenever they met. Then she took to absenting herself for a day or two and we were not surprised to learn that she eventually left the house one day and did not come back.

Never before or since have I kept an animal caged for as long as our wild cats—nine months—and these beasts of all our British mammals are the least suited to confinement. Their spirits often break when freedom is denied them, moreover they are difficult creatures to keep in good health.

So interested was I in these animals that when the female, which had been put in a separate run on Susie's arrival, began to show signs of poor condition and moping I begged Aunt Miriam not to turn her loose—as we had previously agreed to do should either of these symptoms occur in the cats—but instead to try and restore her to her former health and fiery spirits. And my aunt, because of her equal interest in it and my continued pleading, gave a reluctant consent. Usually when a wild animal starts to sicken in captivity from combined ill health and low spirits it is rare for it to recover. What was surprising about this cat and distressing to look back upon, was that for close on five months it suffered from continual ill health, sometimes rallying a little then sinking back into its former weakly state, refusing to touch food and only stepping out into the run for short intervals at dusk. The first thing we did when it started to show signs of a decline was to try putting it back with the male, but he attacked her ruthlessly every time she was reintroduced into the run and so we gave up making the attempt.

One evening I heard piteous mewing coming from her box and on lifting up the top found her lying on her side with her eyes closed, uttering these despairing mews with every outgoing breath. She turned her head round and opened her eyes, looking straight into mine and I saw in them now nothing but pain and misery; all the old fire had gone out of them and I felt she was too weak to even resent my presence. Filled with contrition, I picked up the box and placed it by the open door of the run so that were she able to summon up sufficient strength she could walk out and gain her freedom. The male cat by then was also in poor health, though his condition was not so serious as the other's. I opened the door of his run too and walked away. I did not see him go but in the morning his cage was empty. I chanced to be looking from a croft window, however, when the female left and I saw her walk with extreme slowness from the box, her thick untidy fur fluffed out from her thin body by the wind, her head held down. She continued to walk forwards for several yards, not glancing to right or left, and then sank exhausted among some tufts of grass. I continued to look out of the window at frequent intervals to see whether she had moved, until the small grey form was erased by the deeper grey of dusk. There was nothing we could do for her now except leave her alone undisturbed. Next morning when I went to search for her she was lying dead in the same spot. This experience had the effect of confirming in my mind a fact to which I had previously been veering—t*hat for no purpose whatsoever should a bird or animal be caged except for the briefest periods.* Since the death of the female cat I have always acted in accordance with this principle.

Over to the north-west of the croft lay a series of hills, covered by grass and scree which are so common in Sutherland. Beyond them lay a somewhat higher hill, the lower slopes of which were covered with coarse grass, this in turn giving place to heather. The heather continued to grow abundantly down the far side of the hill which led onto a brief moor. Here were pools of bright green grass set among the ling, rushing burns, silver birches and quite an extensive pine wood. I was particularly fond of this stretch of countryside and hardly a week went by during the summer months when I did not visit it. There was a certain quality, a uniqueness which set it apart from the lower surrounding hills and the mountainous country further to the west. In late summer when the purple heather was in flower the contrast between these few acres and those surrounding them was even more noticeable, for the hills below would be bleached to a dull russet and on hot days the loose scree would burn through one's shoe leather like glowing coals. Nor did the boulders on their slopes offer adequate shade from the sun's beams. But in the pine wood the branches flung out great patches of shade, splashed here and there with brilliant sun spots, the colours of the moor—purple, dark and light green and clear russet of stream and bracken fronds turning golden—were the more appreciated because of their sober setting. On these warm days the pungent reek of pine resin from the wood could be smelt for miles.

I was not the only one attracted to this vicinity; a large number of birds and animals were drawn to it too. In the relatively small area of this favoured spot I have witnessed more wild animals going about their daily business than in any other part of Britain. On several separate occasions I have seen wild cats here. In all, I have only seen these beasts in their natural state eleven times, the other occasions being in totally different parts of Scotland.

Once, when I was resting in a grass ring on a particularly hot day, the heat mitigated by a slight breeze which was blowing towards me, a pair of cats emerged from a hole under a rock which was lying a few yards below me. They both stared at me without any trace of nervousness, then disappeared down a narrow heather run which led on to a patch of scree. Here they turned and looked at me again before continuing forwards with slow, deliberate paces.

I never came across these cats without experiencing a slight feeling of apprehension mixed with pleasure at the encounter. If I were asked to define this apprehension more fully I would say that it springs more from the quality of mystery which is posessed to a greater or lesser degree by all the cat tribe, than to the extraordinary ferocity this species can exhibit when attacked, or to their inborn dislike of humankind. I experienced this feeling to a considerable degree on encountering a wild cat during the last winter we spent at the croft. It was a severe one with heavy falls of snow and strong gales blowing.

There is something exhilarating about being out when one of these gales is sweeping over the hills. And so I set out one day when the snow was lying only on the tops of the higher hills, ostensibly for the pine wood but in fact not really considering getting beyond the first two low hillocks, the force of the wind being sufficient to knock a person over should he lose balance a little.

Clouds unfurled in the silvery sky as they were blown to the south. Walking against the wind, I tucked my chin into my collar and attempted to gain headway. Whenever I reached the shelter of a rock I would rest in the lee a moment in order to gain breath before battling onwards. For several miles the only trees in view were a few scattered birches which bowed and rose at the touch of the wind like swimmers breasting huge waves. These supple trees are seldom much damaged by even the fiercest gales. Except for the boulders, everything was or appeared to be in motion; clouds, birches, even the hills which rolled away to the four horizons did not convey immobility but a smooth movement forwards and outwards. The fascination of this barren scenery I find hard to describe but much of its fascination lies in this very barrenness which impels continuous awareness of the sky as well as the earth. Here one senses a great freedom of the spirit. One does not yearn for a variety of scene where there is space.

Going down a declivity, sheltered from the wind, I unwittingly interrupted a curious little performance given by an ermine (stoat in summer). The grass, because of the nearby burn and the sheltered position, had retained its spring greenness. Against this bright green carpet sported a cream-coloured ermine with the usual black tail tip. It was leaping and prancing with abandon. When they are at this game it generally means that they are trying to decoy prey, keeping a puzzled bird or beast watching in uneasy astonishment as they perform acrobatics worthy of a Chinese tumbler, flicking their lithe bodies, springing into the air, leaping all the while nearer and nearer until they suddenly make a dash and seize the unwise onlooker. In this case there appeared to be no other creature about which the ermine was attempting to capture by this odd performance. Perhaps the noise of the wind had excited him, filling him with the urge to somersault and twist his body into a variety of contortions as he flickered through the air at a tremendous pace. I only managed to witness seconds of his performance before the ermine became aware of my presence and sped down a rabbit hole.

(In Canada and other countries which experience very severe winters, the coat of this animal changes to a pure white and the pelts fetch good prices in the fur markets. In our northern counties this pure white is never attained and the pelts are therefore virtually worthless.)

As I walked the wind slackened somewhat and I managed to reach my objective.

Inside the wood all seemed still and silent after the roar and movement outside created by the wind. It was much darker too and some time elapsed before my eyes adjusted themselves to the dim light. But there was nothing at all gloomy about this wood set on the high moor. The interlacing branches were thick enough to keep out the wind. The ground was almost bare of undergrowth so it was easy enough to walk around the trunks unmolested by briar or strands of ivy. I had brought with me a linen bag in which to put fir cones. When it was filled I started to wend my way through the wood to the far end. My feet sunk in inches of fallen pine needles. Every so often I would swing a branch away from my face and a twig would snap underfoot. My progress was by no means quiet. I walked under an overhanging branch, which just glanced the top of my head, and as I did so I became suddenly conscious of being watched. At the same time I knew the unpleasant sensation of chills running down my spine.

Taking a few paces forwards, I looked about me but saw nothing. The feeling of being watched persisted so strongly however that I continued to gaze nervously about, ready to sprint through the wood at the drop of a pine cone. Then my eyes lighted on the branch under which I had just stepped and I saw stretched along it a wild cat, the largest I have ever seen, though perhaps under the circumstances I may have overestimated its size a little. The creature was gazing at me with an intentness combined with an aloofness but not, so far as I could see, the least trace of fear. Its large luminous green eyes seemed to exert a slightly hypnotic effect over me, for though I was in no mood to study it further—being by now in a considerable state of jitters—I found myself walking a step or two and then, against my will, turning round to have another look at it. And each time I did so it was in the same position on the branch watching me with that curiously remote yet intent gaze.

Another mammal besides the stoat, which changes the colour of its coat during winter, is the blue or mountain hare. The black ear-tips are retained but quite frequently the change from the blue summer coat to the white winter one is only partial.

Blue hares are as erratic as brown hares in their behaviour and are liable to act in an intelligent way one moment, and the next in such a fashion that the most nit-witted hen appears clever in comparison. I have caught blue hares with my hands, as have many others who have lived in the Highlands. A hollow in the ground is extended by the hare, though seldom to any considerable depth, and if it catches sight of one of its numerous enemies it will disappear down this earth. All that is necessary to extract one is a pair of fairly long arms. Generally speaking, the blue hare hides from foxes, stoats, eagles and man under stones and rocks rather than these short burrows. It is a charming sight to see a hare in its white winter coat when the snow is lying on the ground, snug in a snow hollow, fur fluffed out, ears laid back. If something should catch its attention the ears will prick forwards and the hare may stand on its hind legs so as to get a better view. According to the mood it is in, it may streak off over the shimmering snow almost before one has realised it was there, yet on other occasions one may pass within a couple of yards and it will continue to sit snugly in its hidey-hole, apparently quite unperturbed by the close presence of a human being.

Blue hares were very plentiful in our region, yet I have been for a walk and perhaps caught sight of one lone specimen, while later on during the day on another walk I have seen as many as twenty or thirty sitting in the open and at almost every step another would bound away from under my feet.

On a certain day in winter of brilliant sunshine with the snow lying deep and in perfect condition, I came across what I can only describe as a pack of hares. They were gathered within quite a short distance of the croft. If I were to hazard a guess, I would say that there must have been over fifty of them, most of whom had coats turned fully white. From the nonchalant attention they gave me it soon appeared that this was an occasion on which I was presumed safe company. A few hopped out of my way as I approached, others sat almost motionless, their black-tipped ears pricked, several were chasing fellow hares, while yet another would make a quick sprint, as though testing its paces, and come to a sudden halt.

I stood and watched this gathering of the mountain clans, *Lepidus timidus*, for many minutes, and delightful it was. Then a signal seemed to pass among them and on the instant with one accord they sped away with incredible swiftness across the snowfields, their immensely strong hind legs—longer than those of the brown hare's—thudding out a tattoo on the crisp snow. I did not feel that sudden fear of my person or of a suspected animal foe had anything to do with this flight. I believe that they were probably set to move to another region and the signal was given for the departure. Hares usually move any distance in company with several others rather than singly or in pairs.

Having seen two hares hopping about on the snow-covered croft wall with what I took to be hungry expressions on their faces, I picked a carrot from the box, chopped it up and threw the pieces in their direction. They streaked off but I did not doubt that they would soon be back to eat the offering. To my surprise, when I next looked again to see if they had returned there was a fox greedily chewing up the last of the carrot slices.

An amusing episode connected with these animals will give an idea of the strength of their powerful hind legs. It happened whilst Susie's owner was staying with us. We were walking together over the hills when we saw a hare a short distance away disappear down a burrow. Telling her to watch, I placed an arm inside and to her astonishment brought out the hare by its ears. Then I handed over the six pounds odd of struggling, kicking hare, forgetting to tell my friend as I did so to keep it well away from her body. She held it too close and the frightened creature gave her a hefty kick in the midriff with its hind legs which completely winded her for a moment and also caused her to release her grip on it. There was no braised hare for supper that night.

It is generally accepted that, among mammals, the beasts of prey make the most courageous and devoted parents. Having said this, let me straightaway give an exception to this rule by naming the doe of the hare as being a particularly brave and dutiful mother.

The leverets are born in a form of flattened grass in the open country. From birth they are fur-coated and have their eyes open.

In the days when Ben was with us, chasing hares used to be one of his subsidiary activities. When out walking with him Aunt Miriam once had an experience which quite unnerved her for some moments. Ben suddenly darted behind a grass tussock, whereupon there came a loud, agonised scream. He had come upon a form containing three leverets and the doe. It was she who had given this scream as the intruder descended on them and lifted up a youngster in its jaws. After voicing its distress, the doe fled in a wide circle, then stopped, watching the proceedings anxiously as Aunt Miriam endeavoured to extricate the leveret and, having done so, drag Ben away. In spite of the human presence and frantically barking dog the doe proceeded to return, sometimes pausing before coming on farther. She re-entered the form while my Aunt and the dog were still only a short distance from it.

Should a person approach a form without actually discovering its whereabouts, the doe, if she is feeding nearby, will feign indifference or run in another direction, a trick to lure the enemy from it which is common to many birds and mammals.

The hare will only scream when in acute danger or wounded, and it is a distressing cry to listen to, It was this scream that made me resolve to give up plucking them from burrows. On each previous occasion there had been no audible protest from my victims, only a great deal of vigorous twisting and kicking. Then one fateful day—for the local hares—as I pulled one from a burrow by the ears and held it up it uttered a loud scream fraught with anguish which I am sure no actress intent on having the members of her audience reach for their handkerchiefs could have bettered. Gently I placed the hare down by the burrow—which it promptly re-entered—and reached for my handkerchief, vowing as I wiped my eyes and blew my nose that never again would I wittingly cause a hare such distress.

I do not know whether sounds are in fact more audible at night or whether they simply impress one as being so because of the deeper stillness, but it was during the nights that the sounds of the elements and cries of birds and beasts penetrated most deeply into my waking consciousness. They partook of an added quality so that some recognised bird call was imbued with a haunting power to a much greater extent than it had during daylight hours. The dramas which these sounds often told were rendered all the more vivid because of the covering darkness. An owl's notes would strike clearly against the background of silence and dark; from far off the bark of a fox would echo along the corries and be greeted with an answering bark which seemed to come from the other side of the hill on which the croft stood. An otter's whistle down by the lochan would make me wonder as I lay in bed whether Hansel had returned to his former haunts.

On still winter nights when the ground was covered in deep drifts of snow and the air was sharp with frost the sounds would be intensified still further. During my years at the croft the high, fierce cries of the stoats hunting at night never ceased to strike me as being peculiarly sinister. The stoat often hunts in a family party consisting of mother and offspring or larger mixed packs of families and lone stoats banded together. Small though these creatures are, I nevertheless hope that I do not meet up with one of these larger packs when out in the countryside. An indomitable courage and a ruthless ferocity are the two main characteristics of stoats and it has been known for them to attack a human when hunting together.

Well do I remember a cosy winter evening on which we first heard the cries of a pack of these little hunters. We were sitting before the fire drinking Lambs' Wool. This beverage is made by roasting a cooking apple and whipping up the pulp in a glass of hot milk until it is frothy. Sugar and a dash of beer or white wine is then added to taste.

"Whatever's that noise?" Aunt Miriam asked, putting down her glass and going over to the window.

Her ears were sharper than mine and for a while I could hear nothing. Then I thought I detected a faint yelping as from a pack of miniature hounds after its quarry. We were both puzzled by the unusual noise which continued to increase in volume. When the yelps sounded as though they were passing the croft we opened the door and looked out. In spite of there being only a sliver of moon the stars and snow filled the atmosphere with a light sufficient to see distant ranges of hills. A white object sped by followed by a moving mass of tiny darting creatures all following in the wake of the larger object. They, too, were white and it was only after some seconds that we recognised them as stoats in full cry. Our presence in the lighted doorway did not cause them to swing off course a fraction, so intent were they in following their quarry. I could understand how superstitious crofters in the old days often believed a pack of yelping stoats on the warpath to be no creatures of flesh and blood but a pack of demon dogs out to catch the souls of men. Next morning we found the snow to be imprinted with their tracks and the tracks of a hare, stains of whose blood and scraps of fur we found as mute evidence that the stoats had enjoyed a good night's hunting.

Another winter's night we heard above the noise of a gale the unmistakable cry of a storm petrel blown far inland. The cry pierced the lashing wind at intervals and seemed to come from ground level. Thinking the bird had probably met with some harm Aunt Miriam put on a mackintosh and, torch in hand, went out to search for it. By good fortune, she discovered the petrel in the lee of the byre. One of its wings was slightly damaged and so we kept it four days until it was able to take to the air again. Diet was something of a problem as this off-black bird with a white band across its tail normally feeds mainly on crustaceans, but it was not averse to swallowing bits of bread soaked in olive and sardine oil.

A very eerie cry to listen to at nights is that of the wild cat. The long-drawn-out mee-ows have often interrupted my dreams. Much as one wants to fall asleep again, the cry, repeated for minutes on end, holds one bound to the waking world. I think there must have been a rock near us which was much favoured by a particular cat because nights in succession, especially during summer, its cries would come from the same direction, not far off, and continue for as long as two hours on end. Perhaps it kept it up longer on occasions, it certainly seemed so, but one summer night when bars of dark cloud were lying against a sky of deep blue I timed it. The cat woke me up at half-past three. I got out of bed and drew the blinds to, hoping that might make me more oblivious to its sing-song. Then I lay with the bed coverings pulled tight round my ears, trying unavailing to keep out the clear, penetrating mee-ows and envying Lora who, in spite of my movements, and the sounds from without, still slept soundly on her couch. After another prolonged cry had ascended heavenwards there came a faint answering one which made me sit up in bed to listen more intently. And I felt during the long pause which followed that my cat perched on its rock was listening too, every nerve in its body tensed. Once more it set the air vibrating with a throaty mee-ow which this time ended with a peculiar waver as though begging the distant feline to answer again. It did. And so back and forth until just after five-thirty, cry answering cry, those cries of my cat meanwhile growing gradually fainter as it hurried towards the other. When both cries were coming from a distance and then faded away altogether, the sounds of them persisted in my mind for several hours, in the same way as a tune sometimes does, until in desperation I got up, made myself a cup of tea and started to cook the breakfast.

"You were up early. Are you feeling all right ?" Aunt Miriam asked anxiously, it being a most singular event for me to be up before her.

"No," I answered morosely and with what I felt to be small exaggeration; "I'm feeling awful. Two wild cats kept me awake all night."

She studied me closely and then added to my already morose state by saying, "You know, I never did think wine suited you very well. The next time we have Lambs' Wool don't put any in yours. Just make it with plain milk and apple."

a departure and a return

Before Aunt Miriam left for the croft and during the earlier period of our residence there she had been asked, both by word of mouth and in letters, a series of alarming questions guaranteed to put a more nervous person off such a project altogether. "What would you do if...?" they invariably began—"If one of you happened to develop an acute appendicitis, or toothache, or chopped a finger off with the axe?" Another set of questions, equally alarming, but differing from the former in that the possible catastrophe was more in the nature of what insurance societies term an act of God, were of this kind: "What would you do if the roof fell in during a snowstorm?" And there was yet a third category: "What would you do if you happened to be snowbound and ran out of paraffin, or flour...?" or some other vital foodstuff. Quite frankly, I don't know what I should have done if Aunt Miriam had developed an acute appendicitis during a snowstorm.

During our first winter we did in fact run out of various commodities and food items due to miscalculations by Aunt Miriam as to the amounts we should require. But it was no great hardship to retire to bed earlier than usual because paraffin for the lamps was running low, or to exist for a while without sugar.

It was during the last winter that we experienced a more severe crisis, though it was very tame compared to those envisaged by friends blessed with vivid imaginations.

Every autumn among the food items stored for winter use was a large supply of sacks of biscuits for our various domestic animals, the largest consumer of which was Lora. In the days when Ben, the otters and Cuthbert were still with us, getting in and storing a sufficient quantity of biscuits was a weighty problem. The major part of all these animals' diets was biscuits in various forms. We often used to rack our brains to think of a more convenient and cheaper food but without success. Though game abounded, we were without the means or inclination to come by sufficient to satisfy dog, seal and otters. Moreover, changes in the diet of an animal not normally of a domestic nature, such as a seal, cannot be easily made nor made without the risk of impairing its health. Biscuits apart, each species of our domestic animals had its own special dietary extras. It is imperative that a seal should get large quantities of oil, therefore we had to order and cart home tins of edible oil for Lora's benefit. Nuts, practically unobtainable where we were, had to be got in for the squirrels, as well as raisins to act as an occasional fillip to their appetites. Tins of dried milk had to be got in for the otters—we could spare them little goats' milk—and this was mixed with a teaspoonful of oil and a cup of water and poured over the biscuits. But the otters, fortunately—as did Lora—hunted for a goodly portion of their food, otherwise feeding them would have been quite prohibitive.

It was during a spell towards the end of the winter season with snow lying deep round the croft, making a journey to the township out of the question, that I went into the byre one morning to find the two goats looking comatose and evincing the greatest reluctance to walking the few steps towards the spot where they were milked. I put their condition down to the weather and thought no more about it. The following morning their stomachs were noticeably distended and it took more than a few prods to get them to stand on their feet. Then I saw that the tarpaulin covering the stores at the far end of the byre had been pulled out of position and that tins and packets were scattered in chaotic disorder. Investigating matters further, I found that only three bags of biscuits remained intact. The goats had managed to chew through and rip the cloth coverings of the others and devour the contents. Amongst other damage perpetrated by them was the trampling of cardboard boxes containing dried fruit, peas and lentils, stored for human consumption. What remained of these scattered the floor in profusion. A paraffin stove was kept in the byre and on it I melted down a bucket of compressed snow for the goats' and pony's drinking water. Having given it to them, I went to tell Aunt of the disaster. On returning to the scene of the crime Aunt's first action was to seize the bucket and place it out of reach of the goats. One of them had already drunk its fill, the other fortunately was only approaching the bucket for a drink when we entered. We salvaged what we were able from the damaged packages, took out the two remaining bags of biscuits and firmly roped down the tarpaulin round the re-stacked stores.

One bag of biscuits lasted Lora, Sara and Rodney three days, so the supply we had in hand was only sufficient for six days. It seemed highly unlikely that at the end of this time the snow would have disappeared to an extent which would have made a journey to the township possible.

Although Rodney's and Sara's helping of this food was meagre indeed compared to Lora's—one tiny helping soused with milk, in a saucer each evening for the two of them—we nevertheless decided that they must forego their share until we had obtained more bagfuls, and take pot luck, every available biscuit being reserved for Lora.

Once more re-emerging from the byre, I saw Lora, a dark shape, sitting on the flat expanse of frozen, snow-covered lochan, by her plungehole. Her keen eyes spotted me standing on the hillside watching her and she immediately barked a greeting. She missed the company of the otters these days and consequently made more demands upon our time, pleading by bark or look for her ball to be thrown or some other attention.

Looking ahead, the croft behind me, the landscape as far as the eye could see was of a pristine whiteness broken only by the dark shape of the seal. Above the land a grey sky was herringboned by darker grey clouds. It was one of those rare days when hardly a breath of wind disturbed the snow on the hilltops.

Walking down to the lochan, I threw Lora's ball towards her. It proved an excellent shot, ascending in a high arc then falling straight into her mouth, opened wide to receive it. She dropped it into her plungehole and sat watching it. After long moments of utter silence these were broken by a loud bellow of pain coming from the direction of the byre. As Aunt Miriam had anticipated, the goat which had drunk its fill after the night's orgy was now paying the penalty with severe pains, the water having swollen the biscuits and increased the strain on its already distended stomach. The groans and bellowings grew louder and it seemed probable that the animal's life would be in danger if something was not done to aid it. It was led from the byre and, taking a chance, Aunt Miriam poured a strong enema down its throat. This reacted almost at once. The goat was violently sick and some of the pressure on the stomach was thereby removed. Later on came a large dose of castor oil. Although its greed was the means of increasing our labours sevenfold during the following days I could not help feeling as I led the now pitiful looking creature back into the byre that it had fully atoned for its orgy. Food was withheld from both goats the next day and they were henceforth chained to their stalls each evening.

Luckily we still had a good supply of flour for our own consumption and we used it to bake batches of plain biscuits each day. These were mixed with the remainder of the others for Lora's feeds. At the end of twelve days—when we were able to make the journey to the township to collect some more bagfuls—we both felt we never wanted to bake again; indeed we felt an extreme aversion to doing any cooking whatsoever and in order to give ourselves a respite from the stove we lived on milk and fruit for two days.

During the biscuit emergency Rodney and Sara had been living on scraps from the table together with an additional ration of raisins. This change in their diet was much appreciated and the eventual return to plain white dog biscuits soaked in milk was not welcomed. Hitherto both of them had been models of good behaviour whenever a meal was in progress, never pestering the diners for leftovers. Now, owing to the fact that I started handing them down bits from my plate, they grew worse than a pair of badly trained dogs. The saucer of biscuits was left untouched and they applied their wits to getting some more tasty morsel of food, such as they had been enjoying over the last twelve days. To ascend a pair of outstretched stockinged legs is no great feat for either squirrel or rat and if a morsel was refused, nothing daunted, they would proceed to climb up my legs, on to my lap and thence on to an arm and from this vantage point descend—if I was not quick enough to stop them—on to the plate. It is extremely irritating, to say the least, whilst in the middle of a meal, to have a rat and a squirrel running up either leg in the hope of being able to share it with you. Until they were broken of this unfortunate habit it became necessary for me to remember to keep my skirt tucked up and my legs tucked in. When no scraps were forthcoming and no route to the plate negotiable they protested loudly with high-pitched squeaks and chirrups.

When my Aunt went to live at the croft she had no idea of the length of time she would stay there; if the life suited her she intended to stay on indefinitely, if not she would go elsewhere. After seven years, having found contentment and adapted herself admirably to the life, she had no thought of leaving. For myself, aged seventeen, much as I loved the life, I was having to face the prospect of leaving it and to decide—as the majority of young people born to crofter parents do—how I was going to make a living; for it is a sad fact that except in a minority of cases it is virtually impossible to live solely by crofting. As I grew older this problem began to loom ever larger on my horizon, My father, who had been living in India throughout these years, had sent Aunt Miriam an allowance for my up-keep. Not unnaturally, when I reached the age of seventeen he thought I should begin to pay my own way. I asked Aunt, and my father by letter, to let me stay at the croft until the autumn of that year at which season I promised to join the ranks of the earners. To this they agreed and my problem was shelved for a few months longer.

The snow, which had lain deep that winter, had disappeared entirely by early February under a rare spell of sunshine. The weather in March was almost as warm as some of the more bril-liant May days. The young grass had a sheen to it and flowers sprang up in wonderful profusion.

Our first visitors that year were Mr. Fraser and a small niece of his who was staying with them. I spotted the pair of them while they were still several miles distant, the child perched on the man's shoulder, her bright pink woollen dress remaining visible when Mr. Fraser in his more sober attire faded from sight against a patch of scrub or grey rock. This elderly man and the four-year-old child had set out at six-thirty, directly after breakfast, in order to come and see us. The child, so Mr. Fraser informed us, had walked a good portion of the six miles. Neither showed any trace of weariness. On hearing that the goats were still shut up in the byre the little girl, whose parents were farmers, asked at once if she might let them out.

For those who have had much to do with animals it is a matter of moment when a child is brought into contact with one to tell if he is used to their company and if so whether he has been well trained in their handling. Generally speaking, town children evince—naturally—a much greater fear of animals than their country cousins and are diffident and often insensitive in their handling of them. However adroit a child may be in building meccano bridges and so forth, no toy, it seems to me, can compare with having living creatures to play with, and to learn to nourish and tend.

Mr. Fraser's little niece was already an expert in handling animals. She insisted on leading the goats from the byre without any assistance from us. This she did without ado, the goats realising at once from the kindly but firm way she treated them that she would stand no nonsense. A rope in each hand and a goat walking on either side of her, she led them to a patch of turf. The tips of the goats' ears were on a level with the top of her head. She waited for me to stake them and then fearlessly proffered each a carrot in the approved manner.

Watching her with them and seeing the goats' placid acceptance of her as 'master' recalled to my mind an early memory of watching a tiny boy driving a huge pair of water buffaloes along a dusty Indian lane. At a touch from the stick he was carrying, a mere twig, these great beasts of reputedly tricky temperament, lumbered obediently to left or right. This power we have over animals from our early years, a power which is almost taken for granted, still seems to me, when watching such scenes as I have mentioned, as being one of the most amazing man has acquired down the centuries.

Another question frequently posed to Aunt, this time by would-be crofters, was what did she consider to be the minimum sum necessary to run a croft and holding. It is of course not possible to answer such a question at all adequately for others as, obvious truism though it be, what may constitute mental and material sufficiency for one another may find quite inadequate for his needs. And individual requirements apart, crofting conditions vary a great deal in different parts of Scotland and have considerable effect on the economic side. For those who may be interested in this aspect of crofting, I will give a brief list of our main items of expenditure, including various items relating to our own individual requirements.

When my Aunt gave up teaching she had saved sufficient to bring her in an income of some seventy-five pounds a year. Her talents were various and throughout the seven years spent in Sutherland she earned an approximate eighty pounds per annum by painting designs on wooden platters and fruit bowls. The undecorated platters and bowls were sent up regularly by a London store during spring, summer and autumn and were returned by Aunt at intervals during these seasons duly painted in bright colours. Miraculously, the demand for these utensils never seemed to diminish, though even if it had I am sure my versatile Aunt would have found other means of adding to her income. As with the majority of crofters, we were not able to earn anything by crofting, our surplus goods in the way of vegetables and milk being of a negligible amount. Even had we lived near a community and been able to sell this small surplus I doubt if it would have brought us in four pounds a year. It can be taken as true that these days it is not possible to live adequately by crofting unless the main income is derived from other pursuits such as shepherding, fishing, weaving, ghillying or painting wooden dishes.

With the exception of the first year, when among other expensive items a trap and livestock were purchased, we managed to live quite comfortably on a joint income of around £200.

I have made a division in the following list between what can be termed essentials in the general meaning of the word, and those essentials to meet our own particular needs.

	£.	s.	d.
Rates and repairs to croft	7	0	0
Food (other than that grown in the gardens, sugar, flour etc.)	64	0	0
Food for livestock	10	0	0
Clothing	35	0	0
Lighting and fuel	30	0	0
Plants, seeds, etc., for gardens	5	0	0
Extras	20	0	0
	171	0	0
Sheet music and books	12	0	0
Charging of wireless batteries	3	0	0
Food for pet animals	10	0	0
Food for temporary bird and animal visitors	7	0	0
Extras	4	0	0
	207	0	0

Periodically I used to have a certain dream in which I would be lying in a gloomy dungeon, my arms free but my ankles manacled with heavy iron fetters. I was conscious that owing to their weight and because of the length of time I had been wearing them they had had the effect of paralysing my legs. Vainly I would try to turn over but twist as I might, I would find myself incapable of doing so. At about this point something would click in my mind and I would tell myself crossly to stop dreaming such nonsense, that I knew perfectly well the paralysis of my lower limbs was not due to the weight of iron manacles, but to the fact that Lora had sneaked up on to the bed, and was lying across my feet. Awake but firmly pinioned, I would struggle to a sitting position, experiencing as I did so considerable pain from my cramped legs. Ordering Lora off, I would attempt to extricate a toe. The order having been ignored and the attempt proving fruitless, I would next feel for the matches and light the candle. In quick succession I would aim the box of matches at her followed by the pillow. This would have the effect of waking her, but no more, for Lora was made of stem stuff and it would take minutes of tiring pushing and shoving at her person to get her, firstly off my feet, and secondly off the bed. In order to restore the circulation to my legs and feet I would then be compelled to stagger round the room a couple of times.

During the seven years she had been with us Lora had slept each night in my room, as a pup in a cardboard box and later on the bamboo couch. Unlike the otters whose instincts had set them wandering far from the croft until eventually they left us forever, Lora, even if she did absent herself for a day, always returned home to sleep. No dog could have been more faithful or devoted to her human companions than she was. I knew all her small idiosyncrasies. To the last she became very annoyed if I should attempt to play on one of her instruments, which to tease her I sometimes did. If I saw her sitting peacefully outside I would pick up the trumpet and, disregarding the precepts of hygiene except for giving the mouthpiece a brief wipe with a handkerchief, blow a loud toot. Lora would turn round at once and start waddling towards me, grunting her annoyance. Should I continue the tooting the grunts would change to barks and she would tug at my skirt in an endeavour to make me part with the instrument.

In the water I had trained her to follow the boat at command, swim ahead or beside it, or dive underneath without touching it. She would also dive for objects which I threw into the shallower parts of the lochan and bring them up again. When we were going for a picnic on the other side of the lochan she enjoyed carrying the plastic tea-cloth over, swimming on ahead while we, and sometimes Rodney, followed behind in the rowboat. Both of these two mammals were keen picnickers, and when the picnic basket was carried ashore from the boat they would nibble and mouth its straps until the lid was raised. Then Lora would set to work and start the unpacking. This she did admirably, first unrolling and spreading out the cloth, then dropping a plastic cup by each of us. The packets of sandwiches and slices of cake—which were always put inside plastic bags, let me add for the benefit of the squeamish—were placed on the spots indicated. Meanwhile Rodney would be waiting anxiously for these proceedings to end. An occasional stern "Sit!" was necessary if he showed signs of moving in the direction of the fare. Before we started eating, titbits were handed out in the shape of cake crumbs and the contents of a tin of sardines emptied on to a plate.

One day that spring I crossed the lochan in the rowboat and as it slid under the high projecting rock which we called the animals' diving board, Lora, who must have been resting up there, plunged in after the boat, sending up a cascade of water. As I rowed onwards she followed in my wake, swimming in circles round the boat, sometimes on her back. After mooring the vessel I bade her good-bye and set off with my basket in search of wild hyacinths. She was sitting in shallow water, peering over the side of the boat. Her ladder was not fixed to it so she was not able to get in. When I turned round she had started to swim back across the lochan.

That was the last I saw of her. She did not return home in the evening and though we searched and called her name for many weary hours during the days which followed we received no answering bark nor found any clue which might have given us an idea as to why or how she had disappeared. The Frasers and Mr. McNairn kept a lookout for her with no result. Enquiries in the district proved equally fruitless; there had been no strangers or sportsmen about so far as was known and nobody reported a seal venturing down a river which might have conceivably attracted her away with it. And so we never solved the mystery of her disappearance. With her going I lost the closest and most intelligent animal friend I have ever had.

For ten days after her disappearance we kept to the vicinity of the croft in case someone should come with news of her or in case she herself should suddenly turn up. Then, as supplies of paraffin and food were running very low, we harnessed the pony to the trap and set off for the township.

Throughout the early spring we had worked hard in the gardens. The young vegetables were coming along well and we felt assured of a plentiful supply in the near future. These vegetables consisted, together with milk and bread, the main-stay of our diet during spring, summer and autumn.

When we got back that evening dusk was already descending but even in the dim light we noticed that there was something amiss about the place. The wall round the croft garden was broken down in several places and looking over we saw to our dismay that literally every vegetable had been trampled down or uprooted. The pieces of wire-netting with which most had been covered over had also been torn up and kicked aside. From the hoofprints in the soil we realised that a herd of deer had visited the croft in our absence and perpetrated the damage. They had also followed the path from the croft down to the lochan and done equal damage there. A good day's hunting on their part. Deer often do considerable damage to crofters' holdings, but we had been lucky up till then, herds of deer only coming near the croft in winter in the hope of obtaining food.

Aunt Miriam, who was seldom given to fits of depression, found it hard to keep cheerful after this set-back. Lora's going had affected her as much as it had me and with this last bit of bad fortune her spirits became temporarily low. I urged her to go away for a while and to this suggestion she agreed. It was fixed that she stay with friends in far away Berkshire.

"Don't bother to do anything to the garden until I get back," she said before leaving. "Then we'll set to work together."

I took her at her word and spent most of the daylight hours making trips in the canoe up various rivers. During the evenings as I sat in the parlour, alone except for Rodney and Sara, and watched the moths fly in through the open window and flutter round the lamps, the feeling grew in me that the time was fast approaching when we would both leave the croft.

I received a letter from Aunt in which she said that she was enjoying her stay very much and that she and another guest of these friends, a Canadian, had been for some long walks together exploring the countryside. Then came a further letter asking if I would mind her staying on another fortnight. When she eventually returned I received a shock, for she informed me somewhat diffidently that she and this Canadian whom she had met whilst away had decided to get married.

"But Aunt, you can't do that!" I remember saying in astonishment, instead of offering her my best wishes. Somehow it never occurred to me in those days that anyone over the age of thirty-five could seriously contemplate getting married; such is adolescence.

It was arranged that the wedding should take place in three months by which time my father would have returned from India.

So we started to pack. The trap and pony were sold. The Frasers and Mr. McNairn both had a goat apiece and various oddments from croft and byre which we no longer required.

"Well, the morning of your life is over now," said Mr. Fraser as I bade him good-bye, adding, "You will be wandering far in the coming years."

His prediction proved correct for in the years which followed I wandered extensively through Britain and later typed and dish-washed my way up to Iceland where I spent some time in studying a seal colony. On my return to London I felt an impelling urge to escape from the crowds and the noise of the traffic and wander once more among the Sutherland hills, taking a look at my old home. It had been untenanted since we had left it, nobody wanting, apparently, to live in such a remote spot. And so the quest to find a tenant was gradually abandoned. Soon after her marriage my Aunt went off abroad, taking Rodney and Sara with her.

I set off for Sutherland with my camping kit as I wished to camp several days among the hills. In my heart, I felt doubtful about the wisdom of such a trip. Since leaving I had heard that Mr. McNairn had died and the Frasers had moved to a distant clachan, so there would be nobody to visit.

As I climbed the last hill and looked in the direction where the croft had stood I found it hard to credit what my eyes saw. All that remained of our former home was now in ruins and overgrown with nettles. In the five years that had elapsed since we had left it the roof had fallen through, the glass panes had slipped from the windows and the walls were crumbling ruins. Using my rucksack as a buffer, I pushed my way through the nettles and gazed into the room which had once been a parlour. Nettles had even sprung up between the broken stonework. At one side of the room, just as we had left it, was a wooden chair, covered with mildew. Next I peered into my old room. Disintegrated almost past recognition was Lora's bamboo couch, and protruding from under it was a rusted toy trumpet.

The byre was in the same ruined condition. I sat down on a heap of stones, wishing that I had never come. Who would have guessed, I wondered, that the stones on which I was sitting had once enclosed a trim garden?

I decided to retrace my footsteps straightaway. The sight of the croft had depressed me too much to think of erecting the tent and spending the night close by. But as I turned to go my eyes were held by the rolling hills and the dark waters of the lochan; these were the same, as unchanged, as on the day I had first seen them. Then a small incident occurred which raised my spirits further. A thrush flew from the rowan tree and alighted on my shoulder. It was not Breac nor a bird which had been a constant visitor to the croft, but it might have been one of Breac's offspring or perhaps a victim of a winter gale which we had tended for a few days. It sat on my shoulder while I surveyed the familiar landscape, and then as I turned to go it flew off and perched on the ruined building that had once been a home.

afterword
by Maurice Fleming

It is no exaggeration to say that when *Seal Morning* came out in January 1957 it took the reading public by storm. Its publishers, Hutchinson, rushed out one reprint after another to keep up with demand, five in the first year alone. It was, they were soon able to announce, "one of the great bestsellers of our time."

Translation rights had been quickly taken up so that it could be enjoyed by readers in France, Germany, the Netherlands, Italy, Norway, Sweden, Denmark and Japan. It was popular in America too.

Not bad for a simple and comparatively short account of a young girl's childhood—or part of it—in a lonely corner of the Highlands. It was not, after all, as if the writer had any sort of reputation. Rowena Farre was a new and unknown name. She may have once sold an article to a regional magazine, but that seems to have been all.

Rereading it now, after a number of years, I am not at all surprised by *Seal Morning*'s phenomenal success. This is escapism of the best and purest kind. From the first page you are breathing the caller Highland air and soon you are acquainted with a household of delightful pets and savouring the freedom of an uninhibited childhood in a wild and beautiful place.

The writer tells of a life with none of the usual anxieties, cares and petty restrictions of adolescence. The little house on the moor, with its strange menagerie, rings with laughter or drowses in contentment. Who would not envy such bliss?

All of this is reflected in the reviews of the time. Even the London critics were bowled over. John Connell in the *Evening News* hailed it as "an astonishing book, a gem of purest ray, serene…" Nancy Spain declared in the *Daily Express* that it gave her "intense pleasure." In *The Star*, Joseph Taggart said it was "one of the most enchanting animal books for years."

Kenneth Allsop summed it all up in the *Daily Mail*. He wrote that this was "a graceful and essentially honest book. Rowena Farre does not romanticise the wilderness, nor braggingly dramatise the toughness of their Cold Comfort Farm. Yet the plain fabric of their life through the changing seasons makes one's own metropolitan busy-ness seem a shoddy and pointless rat-race."

There speaks the jaded and disillusioned townie!

One might have expected the Scottish book critics to distance themselves a little from all these southern raptures. On the whole they did not. Bernard Fergusson was bold enough to say, "I'm not at all sure that we are not dealing with a minor classic in Miss Farre's book."

The Editor of *The Scots Magazine* was similarly impressed. It had, he wrote, given him "unflagging delight." He continued, "If there is much that is lighthearted and gay in this book, there is also much to tell us how deeply the author entered into the spirit of the austere land…"

He did squirm a little, though, at the author's attempts to reconstruct her conversations with the locals. Readers today will surely agree that Rowena Farre was not good at reproducing Scottish speech patterns.

That quibble apart, the mass of reviewers were united in their enthusiasm for *Seal Morning*. They praised its honesty, its sincerity, its vivid depiction of a Highland idyll.

To my mind the book's appeal is as fresh and immediate now as it was in 1957. The house is as real, the garden, the loch, the path through the heather. The birds and animals are as loveable and unpredictable as when their antics first made me smile.

This in spite of the fact that a rather large question mark hangs over the credibility of the narrative.

Facts about Rowena Farre are thin on the ground. Throughout her life she shunned publicity and interviews. The critics praised *Seal Morning* for its truth and honesty but a study of her second and third books reveal inconsistencies and evasions which must cast some doubts over the first as well.

Her real name was Daphne Lois Macready, an identity she did her best to conceal. By nature she was intensely secretive. In my researches into her life I tracked down Margaret Allan, wife of a retired Edinburgh doctor, who knew Rowena in the services during the war. Lois, she told me, "was a great one for fantasising. You couldn't rely on what she told you."

Mrs. Allan shared a room with Lois on a Radar station for several months but never once did Mrs. Allan get any inkling of her companion's writing ambitions. It was only years later, when she saw *Seal Morning* in a bookshop, with Lois' photograph on the dustjacket, that she remembered how her friend had often sat scribbling.

Lois had talked little of her background or her life before the war, though Margaret Allan understood that, like herself, she had been to boarding school. Her friend never said a word about having spent seven extraordinary years in the depths of Sutherland.

Piecing Daphne Lois Macready's life together is like laying out a jigsaw from which some bits are missing and others faded. This is the nearest I can get to it from the fragments available.

She was born in India, the daughter of an English Army officer. When she was two the family moved to Hong Kong. Four years later her father was posted to Singapore and later to India. From there Lois was brought back to England. She had a brother but little is known of his upbringing or later life.

It was at this stage, if we are to believe her, that Lois was placed in the care of Aunt Miriam, a Scots-born schoolteacher then living and working in the Home Counties. When Lois was ten her aunt retired from teaching and took her niece to live with her in Sutherland. The seven years she claims she spent there leave no time for boarding school, the 'proper education' she undoubtedly received. This is one of the anomalies of the book. In the last chapter she says that, when she left Sutherland, she spent years of wandering throughout Britain and studied a seal colony in Iceland.

In 1942 we have proof from Mrs. Allan that Daphne Lois was a WAAF on a Radar station in Pembrokeshire and this seems to have been followed by a course at a London art school and more travels.

When *Seal Morning* was published she was absent, living, she said, with a group of gypsies. Famously her publishers were unable to trace her and had several thousand pounds waiting in accrued royalties.

She described her experiences with her gypsy friends in her second book, *A Time from the World* (1962). Following this, she again disappeared, travelling, it would seem, to Australia, India and other countries.

166

She returned to Hong Kong and India on a journey which resulted in her third and last book, *The Beckoning Land* (1969). She had become fascinated by eastern mysticism and sought out a guru in his retreat in the Himalayas. Moving into a cave nearby she set herself a strict regime of meditation and abstinence.

What she did in the final years of her life I cannot say but in 1979 this enigmatic woman died at 57. A death announcement of the time said she was the beloved daughter of the late Brigadier John Macready and Marguerite Mary Macready, of Hythe, Kent. The cremation was private and there were to be no letters or flowers. A brief obituary stated that she had not been in touch with her family since 1953.

She left behind three outstanding books and many unanswered questions. Not the least of these, and still unresolved, is the mystery of the location of the house in *Seal Morning*. Every now and then someone has tried to identify the spot. Because she was 'missing' with the gypsies when the book came out, no reporter or other enquirer seems to have had the opportunity to ask her about the house, Aunt Miriam, or indeed any aspect of her sojourn in the North.

She continued to be elusive throughout her career. One has to remember that the media then were nothing like as intrusive and pervasive as they are now. It is most unlikely that even this most secretive of persons could have retained the same privacy today.

The careful reader may have picked up, in her narrative, clues as to the whereabouts of the *Seal Morning* country. It evidently lies well inland from Helmsdale and Brora somewhere between Strath Brora and Ben Armine. A look at the map shows that this is wild country and settlements are few and scattered.

In answer to my enquiries, people who know the area have come up with several suggestions for the location of the Macready home: Gobernuisgach, Dalbreck and Cnocan are the most favoured places but there is little to go on and it is doubtful now if any evidence will ever surface.

While some in Sutherland accept *Seal Morning* as a faithful account of a young girl's experiences, others express scepticism. Is it all true? Or only parts of it? You, having just finished reading the story, must make up your own mind.

And after all, does it matter? If some of it is fiction, does that detract from the quality of the writing? Is the book any less enjoyable?

Whatever the truth of it, I go along with Bernard Fergusson. *Seal Morning* is a minor classic.